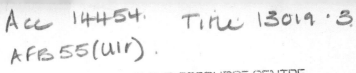

Asian LEADERSHIP

*A*sian
LEADERSHIP
What Works

Edited by

Dave Ulrich
Robert Sutton

Singapore • Boston • Burr Ridge, IL • Dubuque, IA • Madison, WI • New York
San Francisco • St. Louis • Bangkok • Kuala Lumpur • Lisbon • London • Madrid
Mexico City • Milan • Montreal • New Delhi • Seoul • Sydney • Taipei • Toronto

Asian Leadership: What Works

Higher Education

Cover image © iStockphoto.com

10 9 8 7 6 5 4 3 2 1
CTP BJE
20 13 12 11 10

When ordering this title, use **ISBN 978-007-108430-7** or **MHID 007-108430-4**

Printed in Singapore

Contents

Contents

Contents

Contents

Foreword

O ver the last two years, the world experienced one of
its worst financial and economic downturns, prompting
further shifts in the power balance among "traditional"
economies. Outpacing the industrial countries, Asia has
rebounded swiftly from the recession and is poised to be
the key driver of global growth in the coming decades.
Global and regional companies are seeing strong growth
opportunities in Asia. This has led many companies to
bolster their leadership capabilities in Asia to strengthen
growth strategies, including an extensive understanding of
the talent and business landscape. At the same time, the
challenges of leading in Asia have become more pronounced
than anywhere else in the world.

Amidst the increasingly competitive business environment, evolving legal and regulatory frameworks, and rapidly
changing expectations of a more diverse workforce, leaders
need to develop new ways to acquire talent and build a
strong leadership bench strength. Hence, effective leadership
calls for a deep understanding and masterful address of the
unique business, cultural, geographic and human capital
challenges in Asia. Investment in leadership and talent
management becomes a vital competitive factor for growth

and sustainability, and the nurturing of the next generation leaders become ever more critical.

Asia's diversity and growth opportunities present a challenging — yet exciting — context for business leaders and Human Resources practitioners crafting long-term manpower requirements and strategies across the region. Human capital practices and human resources solutions from the West may not be readily applicable in the Asian context. Asia needs to continue to develop its own set of thought leadership and strategic people practices.

Singapore is well positioned to play a pivotal role in creating opportunities for leadership and human capital management development, and driving thought and practice leadership in Asia. Many global companies see Singapore as a choice location in Asia to manage their pan-Asian operations. Asian enterprises also view Singapore as an ideal platform to grow their businesses regionally and internationally. In addition to Singapore's central location in the heart of Asia, the presence of global companies who have chosen Singapore as a regional headquarter and the diverse global workforce, have helped to strengthen Singapore's understanding of Asian markets and their human capital challenges.

Singapore has been playing a role to further thought leadership and strategic platforms for companies seeking Asian solutions for their human capital challenges. The Human Capital Leadership Institute, established as an institution centred on thought leadership and talent development, will generate innovative talent management ideas, practices and strategies contextualised for Asia, in Asia. The Singapore Human Capital Summit, organised by the Singapore Ministry of Manpower and the Singapore

Workforce Development Agency, is a strategic confluence of global and regional business leaders and Human Capital thought leaders who gather to discuss latest trends, thinking and practices in managing and developing leadership and human capital in Asia.

The Executive Roundtable started as an initiative to facilitate strategic conversations among top corporate and thought leaders on human capital and leadership development. These sessions provide a springboard for new ideas and insights that go towards identifying a set of Asian leadership challenges and capabilities, as well as solutions to address these challenges. The first book, *Leadership in Asia: Challenges and Opportunities*, was published in 2009.

This second book, *Asian Leadership: What Works*, which consolidates the main ideas from a March 2010 Roundtable, focuses on practical lessons and experiences of leadership, including what a leader should know or behave to navigate effectively in the Asian market. Eighteen CEOs, Chief Human Resources Officers and thought leaders congregated to deliberate on how the practice of leadership had led to positive differences and impacted business outcomes for their organisations. The Roundtable also generated new perspectives on critical leadership capabilities for Asia and strategies to address pressing leadership and talent management challenges.

I would like to extend my appreciation to the business and thought leaders for their valuable contributions to the thought leadership in Asia on this important topic, and for their commitment to this book. I would also like to express my sincere gratitude to Professor Dave Ulrich, Professor of Business from Ross School of Business, University of Michigan and Professor Robert Sutton, Professor of Organizational

Behaviour from Graduate School of Business, Stanford University, who masterfully facilitated the Roundtable and devoted their commitment in editing this book.

I hope the rich and diverse experiences shared by the corporate leaders in this book will not only be insightful and compelling, but also provide practical wisdom and advice for leaders in Asia to become more effective in developing human capital and business strategies to capitalise on the new wave of opportunities in Asia.

Loh Khum Yean
Permanent Secretary
Ministry of Manpower, Singapore

List of Contributors

DAVE ULRICH is a Professor of Business at the University of Michigan and a partner at the RBL Group, a consulting firm focused on helping organisations and leaders deliver value. He studies how organisations build capabilities of speed, learning, collaboration, accountability, talent and leadership through leveraging human resources. He has helped generate award-winning databases that assess alignment between strategies, human resource practices and HR competencies.

Ulrich has published 20 books and over 100 articles and book chapters. In addition, he has also consulted and done research with over half of the Fortune 200 companies. He is also a Fellow in the National Academy of Human Resources and is co-founder of the Michigan Human Resource Partnership.

ROBERT SUTTON is a Professor of Management Science and Engineering at Stanford University. He is co-founder of Stanford's Center for Work, Technology and Organization, the Stanford Technology Ventures Program and the Hasso

Plattner Institute of Design. He is also an IDEO Fellow and Professor of Organizational Behavior (by courtesy) at Stanford's Graduate School of Business.

His books include *Weird Ideas That Work*; *The Knowing-Doing Gap*; *Hard Facts, Dangerous Half-Truths and Total Nonsense*; and *The New York Times* bestseller, *The No Asshole Rule*. His latest book — *Good Boss, Bad Boss* — was released in September 2010. Sutton's honours include selection by Business 2.0 as a leading "management guru" in 2002, the award for the best article in the *Academy of Management Review* in 2005, being named as one of ten "B-School All-Stars" by *BusinessWeek* in 2007, and the Industry Service Award from the Stanford Engineering School in 2010. His blog, *Work Matters, is at www.bobsutton.net*.

 DEBASHIS CHATTERJEE is the Director of the Indian Institute of Management in Kozhikode and has taught leadership at Harvard University and at the Indian Institutes of Management in Lucknow and Calcutta for more than a decade. He has been awarded the prestigious Fulbright Fellowship twice for Pre-Doctoral and Post-Doctoral work at the Kennedy School of Government at Harvard. His publications include *Leading Consciously* and *Break Free*, which have been translated in several languages, as well as his latest book, *Timeless Leadership*, which will be published in 2010.

Chatterjee has trained more than 10,000 managers globally in Fortune 100 Corporations and has served as leadership coach to CEOs. A pioneer in the field of Asian models in leadership, Chatterjee has served as Dean of an international Business School. He also serves on the Board of Henkel in India as well as Aegeis International.

 LUCAS CHOW joined MediaCorp as CEO in December 2005 and also sits on its board of directors. He started his career with Hewlett-Packard and spent almost 20 years there before joining SingTel in 1998. Under Chow's leadership in MediaCorp, major initiatives in the digital space were launched. These included High Definition TV broadcast, Internet radio, radio applications for mobile devices and a highly successful one-stop entertainment portal, *xinmsn*. Greater emphasis has also been placed on new content formats and joint content production with neighbouring countries. He is also the prime mover of MediaCorp's corporate social responsibility programme.

Chow chairs the Singapore Health Promotion Board and also sits on various boards of directors and advisory committees. He is a member of the National University of Singapore's Board of Trustees and chairs its Entrepreneurship Committee. He continues to be closely involved with the telecommunications sector as an independent director of Emobile Ltd, a Japanese telco services provider. He graduated with a Bachelor of Science (Honours) from the University of Aston, Birmingham (UK).

 CORDELIA CHUNG was named Regional General Manager of IBM ASEAN in January 2009, overseeing IBM's regional operations across Southeast Asia that include sales and distribution, manufacturing, procurement, global delivery and support functions. She joined IBM in 1991 as General Counsel for China and Hong Kong, and was promoted to Vice President and General

Counsel for Asia-Pacific in 1996. She moved to a business leadership role in 2001 with her appointment as General Manager of IBM China/Hong Kong and has since served in various key leadership positions, including Vice President (Business Partners) and Vice President (Financial Services Sector) for IBM Asia-Pacific.

Prior to joining IBM, Chung practised law with an international law firm from 1983 to 1991. She specialised in corporate commercial law and in advising foreign companies doing business in the emerging markets. She serves as a member of the IT Working Group of Singapore's Economic Strategies Committee.

 STUART L DEAN is the President of General Electric (GE) ASEAN. He graduated from Duke University in 1975 with a BA in Economics and Political Science, and received his MBA from Harvard University in 1979. He then joined GE as a Sales Representative for Major Appliance and TV Products. Prior to GE, he worked for the US Government. In August 1991, he was named Business Development Manager of GE International based in Singapore with responsibilities for Southeast Asia and Australia. In 1993, he became President of GE Capital for Southeast Asia. In February 1995, he became President of GE Indonesia based in Jakarta.

Currently, Dean has responsibility for all of Southeast Asia and resides in Kuala Lumpur, where he is a Governor of the Malaysian American Chamber of Commerce. He serves on the boards of the Fulbright Commissions in several Southeast Asian countries and the boards of advisors for the Global GE Community Foundation, US Indonesia Society and the American Chamber of Commerce in Singapore. He is also an active GE Community volunteer and led a week-long home building project in Aceh.

PIYUSH GUPTA is the CEO and Director of DBS Group Holdings and DBS Bank Ltd. Prior to joining DBS, Gupta was CEO of Citibank for Southeast Asia-Pacific, Australia and New Zealand. He serves on the boards of The Institute of Banking and Finance, Global Indian Foundation, Dr Goh Keng Swee Scholarship Fund and Master-Card Asia/Pacific, Middle East and Africa Regional Advisory Board. He is an advisory board member of Sim Kee Boon Institute for Financial Economics and is also a member of the Governing Council of the Human Capital Leadership Institute.

DEB HENRETTA is Group President, Asia for The Procter & Gamble Company (P&G). She is responsible for its $15-billion business spread across key markets like China, India, Japan, Korea, Australia and the ASEAN countries. She was instrumental to the redesign of how P&G does business on this diverse continent by creating a One Asia organisation for P&G that optimises scale by following this principle: "As common as possible; as different as needed."

Henretta is an active participant in discussions on Asia and is a Board Member of the Singapore Economic Development Board and the Business Council of Asia-Pacific Economic Cooperation. She was recognised by the Singapore Government for her contributions with the Public Service Medal in July 2010. In 2009, she was listed at Number

19 on *Fortune's* list of "Most Powerful Women in Business — International".

MICHAEL JENKINS has been serving as CEO of Roffey Park Institute since early 2009. He regularly contributes at conferences on leadership-related topics and has a keen interest in global leadership and talent management issues. He has held several senior positions including Regional Director for Japan and Korea, INSEAD and Director of INSEAD Executive Education Asia, Managing Director and Vice President of Center for Creative Leadership (CCL) Asia Pacific. He started his career as a motor industry analyst with Toyota, becoming its first British employee in Japan.

He holds a degree in Chinese Studies from Durham University and studied Japanese history, politics and economics at Nanzan University on a Rotary Foundation Scholarship.

PHILIP NG is the CEO of Far East Organization, a family-owned property development and investment group operating in Singapore and Malaysia. He is also the Executive Chairman of Orchard Parade Holdings Ltd, the Organization's listed hotel arm and a Director of Hong Kong-based Sino Group, which is Far East Organization's sister company engaged in real estate activities in Hong Kong and China.

He holds a Bachelor of Science in Civil Engineering with First Class Honours from King's College, London University (UK) and two Master's degrees from the Massachusetts

Institute of Technology (US): Master of Science in Technology and Policy, and Master in City Planning. He is the Chairman of the Singapore University of Technology and Design's Board of Trustees and also sits on the Governing Board of The Lee Kuan Yew School of Public Policy.

 HOWARD THOMAS is Chair and Dean of the Lee Kong Chian School of Business at the Singapore Management University. Howard was previously Dean of the Business Schools at Warwick University (UK) and the University of Illinois at Urbana-Champaign (US). He is a distinguished and highly cited scholar in Strategic Management and is the author of 30 books and over 200 articles in his field.

He is a Fellow of the Academy of Management (US), British Academy of Management (US), Strategy Management Society (US) and Institute of Directors (UK). He has been Chair of the Board of AACSB International (US), GMAC (US) and the Association of Business Schools (UK). He has consulted widely for a range of public and private sector organisations in the UK, US and Europe in strategic management, organisational change, risk management and strategic decision making. He is a non-executive director of State Farm Bank, a subsidiary of State Farm Insurance (US).

To the imaginative and hardworking professionals at the Singapore Ministry of Manpower, particularly Arina Koh and Serene Teh

Asian
LEADERSHIP

Prologue

What Effective Leaders in Asia Know and Do

Dave Ulrich
Robert Sutton

As the world recovers from the largest global economic recession and crisis in the last 70 years, Asia is clearly leading the way. Asian countries lead the world in economic growth. China and India are the target markets for both consumer goods and the source of capital for global investment. Other Asian markets are routinely listed among the next emerging markets: Indonesia, Malaysia, Philippines, Singapore, Thailand and Vietnam. "Look East" is a common refrain for businesses looking for economic growth opportunities and for capital to fund their growth.

Central to this economic recovery is a more significant renewal. One of the underlying causes of the economic recession was an eroded quality of leadership. Too many leaders fell prey to deadly blind spots and made atrocious decisions because they:

1. Isolated themselves from their constituents rather than staying emotionally and physically connected to those they served.
2. Did not devote enough effort to hiring, grooming and leading their direct reports.
3. Were closed to new ideas rather than yielding to the influence of others.
4. Sought advice and opinion only from those who agreed with them and brought them good news.
5. Tended to be self-absorbed and self-interested more than other-service and other-centric.
6. Acted on short-term, quarterly performance goals rather than long-term sustainability aspirations.
7. Did not devote the time to understand the details associated with key decisions.
8. Were not patient enough to make sure that all the little things required to implement decisions actually happened.
9. Emphasised consumption, in comparison to others, more than production and seeking success in others.
10. Could not bring themselves to consider, let alone plan for, worst-case scenarios.
11. Developed an attitude of entitlement and hubris more than gratitude and humility.

A full economic recovery will not be sustained without a subsequent renewal of leadership. While Asia is accepted and known for leading the way out of the economic recovery, this book suggests how Asia can also be at the forefront of leadership renewal. Without the right leadership, organisations' promises are unfulfilled, economic recoveries are short-term and society's hopes for improvement of the human condition remain optimistic ambitions.

This book offers modest observations, insights and lessons learned from Asian leaders, their teams and their companies. We propose specific ways to renew leadership. These lessons of renewable leadership are drawn largely from the Asian context, but have global applications. We begin with some reminders about the Asian business context, then suggest leadership lessons from Asia businesses and, finally, offer a framework for leadership renewal.

Asian Business Context

The challenge of leadership renewal within Asia starts with understanding some tenets of the Asian business context. We identified 11 that are especially critical to leaders both inside and outside of Asia.

1. Asian Centrality

Asia has become an increasingly central player in global business success. Based on data from the World Economic Outlook database of the International Monetary Fund, Asia has increased dramatically in the share of global domestic product (see Table 1.1).

Table 1.1 Changing shares of global domestic product between 1980 and 2010

Country/Continent	1980 (%)	1990 (%)	2000 (%)	2010 (%)
Europe	29.7	25.0	24.0	21.4
US	22.5	23.0	23.5	19.7
Asia	7.1	9.0	12.0	22.8

The drivers of Asian growth include catching up with modern technology, increasingly sophisticated leadership skills, improved supply chain management, labour productivity, high savings rates — which allow for funding — and a shift from rural to urban living (Beinhocker et al, 2009). Asian growth creates opportunities for selling products or services to new consumers through-out Asia (not just in other markets), for accessing capital and for sourcing manufacturing and technological services.

2. "Asia is Not Asia"

Asian countries differ along a number of dimensions. Jenkins (2004) noted that "one fundamental principle applies in Asia and elsewhere, leadership *(and business)* is not one size fits all." It is as dangerous to group all of Asia together as Europe, Latin America or Africa. Each country has unique social, technological, economic, political, environmental and demographic characteristics that determine market and organisation maturity. For example, there are many striking differences between doing business in China and Japan. In China, for example, the gender gap is substantially smaller than in Japan. A 2007 survey by Grant Thornton International showed that approximately 25% of businesses in Japan reported that women held senior management positions. In contrast, the survey found that over 80% of the businesses in mainland China reported that women held senior positions.

3. Talent Capacity

Many Asian countries and companies will struggle to have enough talent to meet the increased business demands in the coming decades. When talent demand exceeds talent resources, employees will be more likely to change companies. It also means that the best talent will have more choices about where and when they work. The challenge is acute in mainland China, to the point where it is escalating human resource (HR) costs of all kinds, not just because of increasing salaries, but because of increasing recruiting and training costs. The high turnover is fuelled partly by a dynamic where many multi-national corporations (MNCs) are losing people to larger Chinese firms that have recognised the urgency of filling critical roles in areas which they have been inadequate in the past, and are increasingly able and willing to pay top dollars to get the best talent to work for them to close these competency gaps. Meanwhile, leaders of many MNCs are scrambling to raise pay and to make other changes to make jobs more attractive to top talent, but are still left wondering "what else can we do?" given the war for talent they face.

4. Talent Expectations

The next generation of Asian employees will be dramatically different. The new workforce is not as loyal to the company as to the leader, is more comfortable with democratic than directive leadership, wants to know what is going on in the organisation, wants flexibility of time and job opportunities, expects the organisation to develop them and needs more face time from their leaders (Avolio and Ong, 2008). For example, the new workforce in Thailand prefers leaders who consult more and provide authoritarian directions less compared to prior generations of employees (Yukongdi, 2010).

5. Rural to Urban Population Shift

Across emerging economies, people relocate for jobs from rural communities to urban centres. This puts increased pressure on public agencies to provide services for larger and more dense populations, and greater demands on building the social infrastructure for education, transportation and urban lifestyle.

6. Hierarchical and Deference Culture

In most Asian countries and companies, there is a culture of deference within the hierarchy and an emphasis on teamwork and conformity to shared behavioural expectations. Outspoken employees who challenge their superiors are rare and, traditionally, such behaviour is discouraged. As Hsieh (2006) said:

> "We shift and share responsibility and the fruits of our collective labor. So by standing up you're getting ahead of the field and that's no good. Harmony and hierarchy work to conspire against taking the initiative, which is a big issue in Asian leadership."

7. Collaboration

Asian culture encourages collaboration, mutual support and banding together to achieve common goals — goals often crafted by superiors. Differences of opinion are seldom encouraged and, if voiced, done so privately and with grace. Public confrontations, including potentially constructive differences of opinion, are discouraged.

8. Assessing Company Performance

As Paine (2010) has suggested, the narrow focus on shareholder value that is often emphasised in Western countries, through the strategy frameworks taught in business schools and implemented in many companies, are incomplete and misleading guides for leaders in many Asian countries, including China. Companies need to be good corporate citizens to a greater extent; they need to demonstrate with their plans and actions that they are committed to helping the communities, societies and nations that are part of, to a greater extent than when, doing business in many Western countries.

9. Business Mix

Asian business is moving from a strong bias to manufacturing to other areas, including services, software development and research and development (R&D) activities (Tan and Wellins, 2006). Moreover, some Asian nations, such as Singapore, have long thrived as a result of their commitment and expertise in non-manufacturing areas. For example, Singapore Airlines, Asia's premier carrier, has implemented a strategy of providing superb service while, at the same time, run a cost-effective operation.

10. Relationships

Chow (2005) discusses the importance of *guanxi* or "good connections". Relationships matter as much or more than technical expertise. Many of these relationships are forged through extended family ties, in education or early in careers. Paine (2010) emphasises that relationships with government officials and agencies can be especially crucial.

11. Organisation Types

There is an increasingly clear mix of types of companies doing business in Asia. Three types of organisations have been identified:

1. *Privately-owned enterprises* (POEs). The smaller start-up companies are often run by families. Some of these companies have grown quickly and shifted from family to professional management, but they still have embedded family cultures.
2. *State-owned enterprises* (SOEs). Large, government-owned enterprises govern the traditional infrastructure (construction, telecommunication, education, utilities and finance). These organisations work to adapt to changing conditions and to make the bureaucracy more adaptable.
3. *Multinational corporations* (MNCs). Large organisations headquartered outside of Asia and doing business in Asia and Asian organisations seeking to do business in the rest of the world have the challenge of adapting practices from one geography to another.

For Asia to expand, each of these three organisation types needs to be adapted to become both more efficient and effective.

Conclusion: Asian Business Context

Welcome to Asia. Behind the visible and unique customs and lifestyle are some general principles that shape business context. Those who want to participate in Asia need to recognise these principles; those who want to go from Asia to the rest of the world need to understand their biases as they work in the rest of the world.

Leadership Gaps from and For Asian Businesses

No one doubts the importance of leadership in facilitating business success. The quality of leadership within an organisation affects employee productivity, an organisation's capacity to implement strategy, customer share, investor confidence and community reputation. Research by Gallup on US organisations in both the private and public sectors, for example, shows that those with higher proportions of skilled managers in comparison to similar organisations enjoy greater employee engagement and motivation, and superior long-term performance. As Asia grows and responds to the business challenges outlined above, leadership is a key. For example, McKinsey research suggests that over the next ten to 15 years, China "will need 75,000 leaders who can work effectively in global environments; today they only have 3,000 to 5,000." (Tan and Wellins, 2006)

The Asian leadership gap between demand (what is needed for leaders) and resource (what is available) is large in both numbers and style. The number of required leaders is increasing simply because of the enormous growth. This challenge is further complicated by the demographics of leaders in many Asian countries: top local leaders tend to be in their late 40s or 50s, with the next layer in their 20s or early 30s. In China, for example, many people in their 30s and 40s were growing up during the Cultural Revolution (1966 through 1976) and missed out on ten years of education and experience in leadership positions.

Leadership gaps also exist because the next generation of leaders may need to have different skills from their predecessors. Weldon's (2005) study of 172 senior executives in China's SOEs found that while 51% strongly agreed that developing people was one of their company's top three priorities, only 15% felt that managers know how to do this well. This gap persists because these companies have often relied on an apprenticeship programme for leadership development. The leadership skill gap for MNCs is making sure non-Asian leaders can adapt to local Asian conditions, and Asian leaders going to other geographies can adapt Asian ideas to other local conditions.

The Asian context affects leadership, but we should acknowledge that effective leadership is driven by other factors as well. In Figure 1.1, we propose four factors that might affect what leaders know and do: country (e.g., Asian geography), customers, company culture and personal competencies of the individual leader.

We asked a targeted Roundtable of Asian executives and global thought leaders to weigh the relative impact

Figure 1.1 Factors affecting leadership

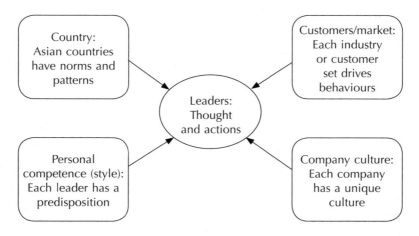

of these four drivers by dividing 100 points across the four. While there was some disagreement among these experienced leaders and experts, the greatest consistency was around the weight placed on country, which received between 15 and 20 points. So, although country mattered in the estimation of these wise people, other factors mattered much more. In particular, customers received far more points among those we surveyed.[1] Effective leadership requires the ability to understand and to adapt to all four factors. Each tempers leadership. Asian flavouring exists, but it must not overwhelm the other, often more crucial, factors.

There is an Asian flavouring, like food flavouring, that affects how leadership works. There are four food groups that have basic food intake, but the food is flavoured differently in different countries. Likewise, there are some basic leadership roles that must adapt to Asian flavouring.

Distinct Leadership Challenges

To fill the leadership gaps, there are distinct challenges in the Asia business context.

Managing Succession

Preparing the next generation of leaders requires that future leaders move beyond technical to leadership proficiency.

---

[1] We have done this same exercise in other settings with similar results, with customer receiving the most points and with country receiving 15 to 20 points.

In some Asian organisations, individuals are often moved into leadership roles because of seniority or being next in line more than being prepared to transit into leadership. Avolio and Ong (2008) called this accidental leadership, where leaders move into their jobs by accident, personal desire, incremental promotions or relationships. MNCs that operate in Asian countries provide a learning opportunity (and a source of talent of local companies) because they tend to have more systematic and merit-based succession systems.

Encouraging Asian Leaders to Balance Execution With Innovation

Asian leaders are sometimes more gifted at execution than creation. Often, the Asian education system encourages more rote learning than innovative thinking (Tan and Wellins, 2006). This execution focus fits with a business focus on manufacturing and operations, but the need for innovation increases with the increasing emphasis on R&D and marketing.

Replacing Expatriates With Local Leaders

In almost all emerging markets, companies enter the market with expatriates who bring leadership depth and experience, but lack local sensitivities. In emerging Asian markets, many companies seek to develop local leaders for local situations. This requires rapid leadership acceleration where younger and less experienced leaders can quickly learn the requirement of leading complex organisations (Jenkins, 2006).

Retaining Talent

As noted, when the demand for leadership exceeds supply, leaders (and other employees) have great flexibility in where they work. One study of Chinese leadership showed turnover at about 20% per year, which limits organisation sustainability (Jenkins 2006). A recent *Harvard Business Review* article featuring interviews with expatriate executives in China found that over 50% reported that retaining top talent was among their top challenges, even during the financial downturn in 2008 and 2009. Retaining talent means finding an enduring employee value proposition that includes money, but goes beyond it to helping employees find meaning at work (Ulrich and Ulrich, 2010).

Engaging Employees

Retention is not just about opportunity. It also comes because some companies have low employee engagement practices. Mercer Human Resources Consulting shows that Chinese employees rated "involvement and engagement" less favourably than almost all other aspects of their work environment. According to a Towers Perrin survey, only 8% of Chinese employees are highly engaged. Only Japan scored lower on a list of 17 countries (Tan and Wellins, 2006).

Investing in Leadership Development

Research shows that about half of all leaders (47%) feel organisations do a "poor" or "fair" job of leadership development. More than half of global and North American leaders (51% and 55%, respectively) feel formal training is an important component of ongoing success. Unfortunately, according to one survey, only a quarter (26%) of Chinese leaders see it as valuable (Tan and Wellins, 2006). The challenge here, as in all organisations throughout the world, is to develop a long-term commitment to training and developing leaders, and to stick to that commitment especially during financially difficult times; those countries and companies that sustain such commitments during tough time suffer less severely and, when the good times return, have a huge competitive advantage over their competitors.

These leadership challenges are not unique to Asia, but they are more poignant and more pressing in many cases because changes in markets, operational approaches and governance practices are unfolding more rapidly in the region than in any other region in the world. Indeed, perhaps the most pronounced and distinctive pressure that many Asian leaders face is that they are under pressure to learn more, change themselves more and change their organisations more, and to do so more quickly than in any other region in the world. To respond to these challenges quickly and effectively, it is crucial to be clear about what makes an effective leader in general, and in Asia in particular.

Asian Leadership Skills

Given the Asian business context, gap in Asian leadership, the pressures to learn and act fast, and the distinct local and regional challenges for Asian leaders, this book addresses the question: What should effective leaders in Asia know and do?

Others have approached this topic and identified some of the strengths and characteristics of Asian leaders. Based on interview of 44 Chief Executive Officers (CEOs) of Asian organisations, Avolio and Ong (2008) have identified strengths of Asian leaders, that is, they:

1. Are highly confident.
2. Are generally aware of how they impact others.
3. Are more likely to listen first before acting.
4. View their top management team's skills, experience and commitment as an organisational strength.
5. Are results-oriented.
6. Will support leadership development efforts only if they are practical and embedded in day-to-day activities.
7. Are willing to be directive when needed, as opposed to simply being participative and collaborative.
8. See integrity as one of the most important values of leadership.
9. Spend approximately one day a week informally developing their followers into leaders.

Hsieh (2006), an astute observer of Asian leaders, has noted the high ambition and work ethic among most Asian leaders:

"I have been impressed by two things that Western companies can learn from Asian companies. One is the level of aspiration. Asian CEOs have lofty aspirations and dream big dreams. I wish some Western CEOs would get a piece of that magic. Many of the development problems I talked about, like systematic investment in people, have been overcome just by having incredibly visionary leaders in Asia. In many cases the personal visions of Asian CEOs are less self-centered and more selfless than those of their Western counterparts. The Asian CEO has a very attractive vision because it is for a noble, higher purpose — for society, for the country, for the collective."

This research and expert opinion about the hallmarks of Asian leaders is especially intriguing because it matches so well with a large body of research on the attributes of the very best managers and leaders in Western organisations. The best bosses balance a high level of confidence with a deep awareness of how they impact others. They listen carefully and ask good questions, but then act decisively. They place a premium on implementing good ideas, not just planning and talking about them. They take a long-term perspective, acting like they are running a marathon rather than a sprint. And they consistently put the needs of their organisations and their followers ahead of their own (Sutton, 2010). As such, we are struck by how the typical attributes of Asian leaders sound so similar to the attributes of the very best Western leaders.

In addition to these potential advantages, further evidence that Asian leaders are poised for success are suggested in a study by Development Dimensions International that shows Asian leaders are more committed, fulfilled and ambitious than Western leaders (Tan and Wellins, 2006; see Table 1.2).

Table 1.2 Differences in ambition between Chinese and North American leaders

Variable	Chinese (%)	North American (%)
Satisfied with work-life balance	80	69
Willing to make personal sacrifices	93	66
Desire for promotion to senior level	95	65
Agree with the statement: "work is more fulfilling than my personal life"	45	3
Too much work	23	49

Source: Development Dimensions International

In their study, they also assessed the gap between required skills and the perceived strength of those skills among Chinese leaders. Table 1.3 shows that many critical leadership skills are lacking in Chinese leaders.

Table 1.3 Skills needed versus strength of leaders in China

Skill area	Critical skill needed (%)	Strength of Chinese leaders (%)
Motivating others	80	26
Building an environment of trust	80	25
Retaining talent	75	11
Leading high performance teams	68	16
Building winning partnerships	57	29
Delegating for results	55	32
Leading change	53	14
Achieving leadership potential	49	10
Valuing differences	41	24
Setting performance expectations	40	16

Source: Development Dimensions International

The upshot of these studies and expert opinion is that there is good reason to believe that Asian leaders tend to already possess the mindset, commitment and work ethic to be as good, and arguably much better, than the best leaders in the world. The main thing standing in their way is that many still need to learn and master a core set of fundamental skills. There is also reason for optimism here as well given that, as we will see in this book, many Asian leaders and organisations are already practising and spreading these skills throughout the management ranks. Moreover, there is overwhelming evidence that the skills listed in Table 1.3 — such as motivating others, leading

19

teams and setting performance evaluation — can be learned and then performed at the highest level by any leader who is committed to doing the hard work required to master, and who coached and taught, the proper methods. As we have seen, commitment and willingness to put forth great effort are hallmarks of Asian leaders. And, as we will see in this book, the coaching and teaching in many Asian organisations is already world class.

Asian Leadership Going Forward

The Singapore Ministry of Manpower (MOM) sponsored a leadership Roundtable that was designed to build on existing insights and evidence about leadership in Asia. In particular, participants in this Roundtable focused on what challenges Asian leaders will face going forward and which strategies, tactics and skills would be most crucial for succeeding in the face of these challenges. This leadership focus group comprised corporate CEOs, Chief Human Resources Officers and leadership thought leaders.

The group spent two intensive days reviewing the business challenges, leadership gaps and requirements, and then posited what ideas and actions Asian leaders needed to master going forward. Based on these intensive two days and numerous follow-up conversations, we identified four general questions that leaders in Asia must answer in order to succeed at the highest levels. We also identified eight action domains (i.e., duties and responsibilities) that the executives and thought leaders who attended the Roundtable deemed as most essential to their success, along with the skills required to accomplish these actions. We then captured how these general leadership questions, actions and skills need to be flavoured for the Asian context (see Table 1.4).

Table 1.4 Leadership success factors

Question	Action domain	Skills: A leader must have competence in ...	Asian context: Asian leaders need to manage tensions in each area ...
Where are we going?	Creating customer-centric actions	• Anticipating, responding to, ignoring at times (i.e., the wrong customers and bad ideas) • Shaping customer behaviours and needs, and linking them to internal employee actions	• Serving traditional Asian customers while adapting services to new global customers • Turning external customer demands into internal employee actions
	Implementing strategy	Folding the future into the present, turning aspirations into actions (closing knowing-doing gaps) and moving from big ideas to daily routines	• Having a discipline (rules-driven) strategy process while encouraging innovation • Having grand aspirations for the future coupled with daily actions for today
How do we get there?	Getting past the past	• Adapting, learning from and improving on the past • Forgetting the past when necessary • Creating new patterns (not events) of how work is done	• Respecting Asian cultural norms while competing in a global market • Being able to respect the past while not being unreasonably bound by it

(continued on next page)

21

Table 1.4 *(continued from previous page)*

Question	Action domain	Skills: A leader must have competence in …	Asian context: Asian leaders need to manage tensions in each area …
	Governing through decision making	• Decision making, assigning accountabilities, leveraging size and scale while maintaining personal and community connections • Creating infrastructure to sustain change	• Holding people accountable while working in an Asian, non-confrontational cultural context • Gaining efficiencies of scale and size while maintaining intimacy and customisation of small
What is work like when we get there?	Inspiring collective meaning making	Evoking passion at work, creating purpose-driven and affirming work cultures, melding personal and organisational identity	• Creating a sense of meaning at work while making money • Connecting an organisation's purpose with an individual's personal meaning
	Capitalising on capability	• Building a culture that combines individual abilities into collective capabilities • Accepting diversity and differences while maintaining unity of purpose • Having exceptional people who work well as teams	• Being individually proficient while working well in teams • Supporting constant learning and teaching, and constructive discussion of successes and failures • Maintaining an Asian identity while adapting to diversity of other cultures

Who stays and who goes?	Developing careers	• Helping people set individual and organisation expectations about both specialist and generalist careers • Having T-shaped individuals and careers	• Working as a technical expert (specialist) while being able to work across boundaries (generalist) • Allowing people to explore different paths and to make mistakes, and providing supportive guidance and mentoring along the way • Identifying, clearly expressing and implementing guidelines about the skills and values necessary for advancing in the organisation, and the consequences of not meeting these standards
	Generating leaders	Identifying and investing in next generation leaders	Maintaining a leadership style of humility while being directive and getting things done

We organise this book to answer these four questions by offering deep insights into each of the eight success factors. Each of these eight success factors are briefly described below. These descriptions include the distinct challenges of the Asian setting, the role of the leader, the competencies they must demonstrate, the paradoxes they manage and the actions required to get there. In the eight parts of the book, we will offer a brief insight on each success factor followed by a short case study of a company that works this issue well, and then consider the lessons learned across the companies described in the book and elsewhere from the thought leaders who participated in the workshop.

1. Creating Customer-centric Actions

All leaders succeed when there is connection between customer expectations to employee actions. Asian leaders need to continue to identify and serve traditional Asian customers and, at the same time, become aware of and responsive to emerging global customers. This means that Asian leaders must become aware of potential customers in addition to the customers they serve now and then use those customer expectations to drive internal employee actions. Asian leaders need to spend time with customers in emerging and new markets. They also need to find ways to understand and satisfy the unmet needs of both current and desired customers. By being close to current and potential customers, and developing an understanding of what these customers would be delighted to pay for even if they cannot articulate it at the moment, Asian leaders will be more able to create and satisfy customer expectations, and then link them to internal employee actions.

2. Implementing Strategy

An unimplemented strategy is as useless as having no strategy at all. So strategy is not just about where we are going; it is about how to get there. Asian leaders, like their counterparts throughout the world, need to become gifted at not just making the present better, but at anticipating, innovating and creating a future. Much of the Asian tradition lies in disciplines to accomplish a task. Asian leaders will also need to have the creativity to discern an unknown future and build the agility or capacity to act to get there. Asian leaders also need to master the ability to articulate long-term plans, goals and lofty aspirations, and then link them to the daily actions, small wins and routines that enable those dreams to come true. When employees doing today's work can connect it to tomorrow's opportunities, leaders not only build the right strategy, but they make it real.

3. Getting Past the Past

Almost all human beings are bound by their cultural norms and, as hundreds of psychological studies show, are soothed and comforted by old and familiar ways of thinking and acting, and seeing the world. Traditions and old ways of seeing the world have many advantages as they induce loyalty and often continue to be effective ways of thinking for hundreds, even thousands, of years. But there are also times when such ingrained, old ways become obsolete and downright destructive. Asian leaders who work in countries with strong cultural heritages and norms must learn to thrive under such constraints, to learn how to accentuate the best and dampen the worst of these strong forces. Leaders in such cultures master the skill of respecting traditions without being so strongly bound to them that their company's performance, and their people's well-being, suffers. By their example, Asian leaders will help their Asian employees to both revere and move beyond their cultures. Asian leaders will also help new entrants into the Asian work setting feel respected for their unique contributions, and yet adapt their abilities to the Asian context. These leaders will have flexibility, agility and responsiveness.

4. Governing Through Decision Making

In Asia, to be effective, leaders need to master a distinct perspective about decision making. This perspective requires that leaders learn to make decisions that help their organisations simultaneously leverage scale and size, and deliver on a sense of small and focused. Making decisions also requires building a governance process that deal with relationships (who is involved in the decision), roles (what positions and roles shape decisions) and rationality (what are the criteria for the decisions). As a governor, a leader is able to figure out what decisions need to be made, who needs to make them and how they need to be made. As decision making becomes institutionalised, the leader's organisation is governed in a way that creates value for both employees inside and customers and investors outside.

5. Inspiring Collective Meaning Making

Asian leaders need to become meaning makers. Most Asian employees have the competence to do their work and the commitment to work hard at the work that they do. But to retain top talent and to make sure that top talent is as productive as possible, Asian leaders need to help employees find a sense of meaning or purpose in the work that they do.

When employees believe in their work not only for financial gain, they offer more of their discretionary energy to doing their work well. This means managing beyond skills and rationality, and making sure that employees feel emotionally connected to the company.

6. Capitalising on capability

To be as effective as possible, Asian leaders will need to manage the paradox of individual and collective action. They have to help individuals develop and apply their distinct talents and abilities to do productive and (especially) creative work. At the same time, they have to help individuals work well in collective teams. There are times when Asian employees submit their personal identity to the collective, but doing so undermines the ability to do creative work or to see a complex decision from multiple perspectives. When this happens, Asian leaders need to adopt and invent ways to encourage individual thinking, constructive disagreement and solutions that weave together diverse and perhaps clashing perspectives. At other times, such as when collective action and effort towards a common goal using agreed upon approaches is required, individuals (either from inside or outside Asia) who put themselves above their teams can undermine performance. In such cases, leaders need to build and draw upon collective identity and unified action, and work to stifle and stop actions taken by selfish and destructive solo players.

7. Developing Careers

Asian leaders need to help individuals build and manage their personal careers. Individuals need to find a balance between deep expertise and broad generalist abilities. Skilled leaders help individuals make informed choices about the extent to which they should be specialists or generalists. Leaders also help employees gain relevant competencies that are consistent with their personal choices, values and goals. Skilled leaders also help their organisations manage careers like a "T", where there is an appropriate balance between deep vertical expertise and broad knowledge, interpersonal skills and personal connections inside and outside the organisation. When employees make informed career choices, and when leaders thoughtfully manage careers, organisations have employees who are more likely to be the right people in the right jobs at the right time with the right skills. They are also more likely to have people with deep skills the organisation needs to be as effective as possible in key domains, and the broad knowledge and wisdom to know when those deep skills can help the organisation succeeds (or are completely wrong for the problem at hand).

8. Generating Leaders

Asian leaders have a significant challenge of developing next generation leaders. Leaders (the individual) matter, but leadership (the collection of leaders throughout a company) matters more. Leaders need to replace themselves with those qualified to manage against future, not present, business demands. They also need to be committed to develop leaders who, ultimately, will be more skilled than themselves. This means that Asian leaders who have grown up in one setting may need to develop their successors who can lead in another setting. Managing succession or leadership transition ensures that the organisation is prepared for the future, not just the present. Doing this well not only assures that the organisation will have the right mix of skills to succeed in the present and the future, it also helps assure that the best and brightest leaders will be motivated to stay with the company, rather than leaving out of frustration because their talents are not being appreciated and developed.

Conclusion

The bulk of the world's best resources in the leadership field, as tradition would have it, are still outside Asia. So a pessimist might say that this whole subject of developing leadership in Asia is premature. We prefer a different and more upbeat perspective, especially given the need for so many great leaders and so much great leadership in Asia. Those of us who attended the Roundtable organised by Singapore Ministry of Manpower chose, instead, to see this challenge as a unique opportunity for the world's best leadership thinkers, advisers, counsellors, coaches and academics — and the many great leaders and organisations that have already accomplished so much in Asia — to collaborate and learn. By doing so, we are optimistic that sufficient insight and momentum can be generated so that few Western companies will fail in Asia, and that most native Asian companies can develop the strength to withstand the coming years of breakneck-speed growth and create the leadership capacity to implement the necessary changes.

References

Avolio, B.J. and P. Ong. (2008). *Accelerating the Growth of the Asian Leader*. Singapore Human Capital Summit.

Beinhocker, E., I. Davis and L. Mendonca. (2009). The 10 trends you have to watch. *Harvard Business Review*, (July/August):55–60.

Chow, M. (2005). Are Western leadership development approaches appropriate in China, or might a Chinese approach be more effective? *Leadership in Action*, 25:13.

Ernst & Young. (2009). *Research on Asia: Embedding the Right Managerial Talent in Asian Businesses*. Singapore Human Capital Summit.

Hsieh, T-Y. (2006). Bridging the divide: a conversation with Tsun-Yan Hsieh. *Leadership in Action*, 26:10–2.

Jenkins, M. (2004). A question of leadership. *Leadership in Action*, 24:12.

Jenkins, M. (2006). Managing talent is a burning issue in Asia. *Leadership in Action*, 26:20–2.

Paine, L.S. (2010). The China rules: a practical guide for CEOs managing multinational corporations in the People's Republic. *Harvard Business Review*, (June):103–8.

Sutton, R.I. (2010). *Good Boss, Bad Boss*. New York: Business Plus.

Tan, R. and R. Wellins. (2006). Growing today's Chinese leaders for tomorrow's needs. *Training and Development*, 60:20–3.

Ulrich, D. and W.L. Ulrich. (2010). *The Why of Work*. New York: McGraw-Hill.

Weldon, E. (2005). A question of leadership. *Leadership in Action*, 25:12.

Yukongdi, V. (2010). A study of Thai employees' preferred leadership style. *Asia Pacific Business Review*, 16:161–81.

PART ONE

Creating Customer-centric Actions

2

Banking the Asian Way

Piyush Gupta

When faced with the wrath of nature, most folks would probably throw in the towel, but not Subir Chakraborty, Puneet Punj and Sandeep Kumar. In May 2009, the trio, part of our DBS India team, demonstrated their commitment to customer relationships, come hell or high water — literally.

At the time, DBS' Kolkata branch, a relatively new setup, had approved a multimillion-dollar loan to a client with diversified interests in cement, paper and electricals, and the customer indicated a desire to meet as he needed to draw down the funds urgently.

On the morning of the scheduled meeting, however, Kolkata awoke to fierce torrential rains as Cyclone Aila was about to rip through Eastern India and Bangladesh. On the roads, the scene was one of utter chaos, with incessant rains, fallen trees and traffic jams. Even the approach road to the client's office was sealed off.

With the customer's pressing need foremost on their minds, however, Subir, Puneet and Sandeep braved the unforgiving weather conditions with determination. By the time they arrived for the meeting, the DBS trio made quite an impression. Probably for the first time, our customer saw his bankers dripping wet, with shoes in one hand and documents in another! We may not have won first prize in a fashion parade, but we most certainly scored top marks for our dedication and commitment. Needless to say, the client relationship was solidified from that time on.

Asian Banking

This DBS India story, and many others like it, is often celebrated within the bank because our ambition is to become a bank known for consistently delivering a heartfelt form of Asian service. Asian service, to us, is about "the humility to serve, the confidence to lead".

The year 2010 marks the beginning of what has been heralded as Asia's decade. As Asia rises, banks such as DBS which are born and bred in Asia have a unique opportunity to differentiate ourselves, and to make our mark as a leading Asian bank.

I am convinced that in an industry as competitive as ours, where many products are highly commoditised, we can be a bank apart only if the customer is front and centre of all that we do. We need to put ourselves in the customers' shoes, and to see things from their perspective. Let me share a few examples.

Banks are notorious for communicating with clients in obtuse language laden with financial jargon or legal speak. In extreme cases, a client with a bank letter in hand might be forgiven if he thought he was reading gobbledygook! A client-centric approach would be to demystify banking for the customer. At DBS, we have begun a process of combing through our client communications with a view to simplifying them. Where possible, the bank is also trying to do away with product fineprint, as we did last year with a unit trust advertising campaign. Admittedly, we still have some way to go, but the journey has begun.

While technology has changed the way people bank, not everyone is equally comfortable with electronic banking. Among Singapore's "silver-haired" population, there are still some who prefer to walk into a branch rather than tinker with Internet banking. When we put ourselves in our elderly customers' shoes, we realised that many would feel more at ease if they were served by compatriots from their own generation. So we deliberately launched a recruitment drive among the older folk and today, DBS has about 120 retirees in our POSB branches helping the elderly with their banking transactions.

At the height of the financial crisis in late 2008, as liquidity dried up, the Singapore government enhanced a financing scheme to enable small and medium-sized firms to have continued access to bank credit. DBS strongly supported this scheme. In fact, from December 2008 to December 2009, DBS disbursed the most number of micro-loans, or loans of up to S$100,000, to companies with fewer than ten employees. Smaller players are most vulnerable during such crises. For them, credit can make a huge difference between success and failure. DBS stepped up to help because we understood their predicament, and believe in standing by our customers through thick and thin.

I could go on, but these three examples underline the disparate ways in which a bank like ourselves can do more if we are to be truly customer-centric.

The challenge is that while we have pockets of customer excellence, it is neither consistently applied nor all-pervasive yet. There is much more to be done to embed a strong customer mindset within the bank, and to unleash a tsunami of best practice across the entire organisation.

Empowering our People

So what are we doing about it? In my view, banking is all about HRIT — namely, HR and IT! When we get these two ingredients right, we will be pretty darned hard to beat, especially when they are focused on customers!

On the people front, we seek to give our folks the right training, in both the soft and hard skills. Then we need to empower them, and trust that they will do what is right for our customers.

Jennifer Pardo Tiburcio works at the DBS contact centre in Singapore. In May 2010, she received a hotline call from a customer who needed cash urgently as he was stranded in Nepal. To compound matters, he was almost down to his last cent. The Maoist riots then raging in Nepal had shuttered many shops, and most ATMs and branches were closed. In desperation, the customer called us, even though he knew that DBS has no branches in Nepal, to ask if there was any way he could withdraw cash.

After Jennifer took the call, she tried to arrange for emergency cash through MasterCard International, but was unsuccessful as all the Western Union branches in Nepal were also closed. However, thanks to her resourcefulness, she managed to find out that Standard Chartered Bank had operations in Nepal. She also obtained information about which ATMs remained accessible, and pointed the customer to one in the area where he was staying. This proved to be not only a lifesaver to our customer, but also many other tourists who were similarly stranded without cash.

I share this story because I am sure this scenario was never part of any training session Jennifer had gone through. No training manual can be that comprehensive. In many situations, where our people have to react quickly and make snap decisions, they will be guided by nothing more than the values of the organisation. They have to know that the organisational culture rewards a truly customer-centric approach, even when they are doing something as counterintuitive as referring the client to a competitor!

How will our people know this?

For one, the leadership has to walk the talk. Our senior management have begun spending a few hours in the trenches, serving at branches or at our call centre. Empathy for our service staff, and our customers, can only be engendered when we ourselves interact with people on the ground.

At DBS, we are also committed to launching 50 "Improvement Events" in order to reduce inefficiencies in our processes and the way we do things. By taking out unnecessary steps in a process, we have reduced the time it takes to open a corporate account from 14 days to one day. In Hong Kong, we have also reduced the time to disburse a corporate loan from four weeks to under a week.

Of course, not every initiative is top-down. When you are an organisation of 14,000 people, it takes a chain reaction of end-to-end teamwork — often across units, and sometimes even markets — to deliver true customer value. If one link in the chain breaks, the entire chain breaks. To succeed, we need to harness the collective can-do of our people, and to engage them on how we can improve in big and small ways. We need all of them to catch the vision!

In line with this, in 2009, we launched a bankwide drive for ideas that would spark a customer mindset and culture shift. We received a groundswell of responses from our employees, with a total of 600 ideas generated in Singapore and Hong Kong. Many of these were subsequently implemented.

Harnessing Technology

If people are one part of the equation, technology is the other.

In banking, leveraging technology is all-essential if we are to deliver superior customer service. Take mobile banking (mBanking), for example. We launched this service in April 2010 to cater to Singaporeans on the move, and to make banking more convenient for them. As of July 2010, over 130,000 new users have signed up for mBanking, surpassing all initial expectations.

In March 2010, DBS collaborated with PayPal to allow our four million customers in Singapore to shop online globally, not just with their credit cards, but by debiting their bank accounts. The idea is to provide our customers with as wide a range of payment options as we can.

We are also moving into the social media space. DBS has been actively monitoring online conversations for over two years. Technology and social forces have empowered the individual to act as citizen marketeer, influencer, activist and self-publishing journalist. By monitoring online chatter, we can tap into a groundswell of consumer opinion and transform the customer experience we deliver.

In particular, the younger set seems to prefer to grouse about us online than to provide us with feedback directly. By monitoring what they say in cyberspace, we can glean valuable feedback and address issues we might not otherwise be aware of. Examples of appreciative "netizens" include one who said: "DBS picked up my tweet … and contacted me with fix. Well done."

Going the Distance

To build a competitive advantage and to set ourselves apart as a leading bank requires perseverance. We need to build on past successes and push for future ones. It is a painstaking journey that requires leadership and commitment from everyone in the organisation. It also requires a mindset change, one that demands that every process and detail be seen through the customer's lens. We need the will, discipline and focus to reshape the hardware and "heartware" of the organisation.

It is still early days yet, and there is a lot more to be done. Every day, though, as our people walk through the lobby of DBS Asia Hub, our new office in Changi, they are reminded of what we want to stand for. The source of inspiration: a unique set of sculptures by contemporary Chinese artist Gao Xiaowu. Three of these stylised human figures have their hands outstretched in a warm handshake, two of them bowing in grace. They are a constant reminder to us of what we want to become: a leading Asian bank that is distinct because we bank the Asian way.

Aligning Leadership For Customer Satisfaction

Philip Ng

Creating New Desires

Far East Organization was founded on the entrepreneurial vision of our first-generation leader and founding Chairman, Mr Ng Teng Fong, who saw in the late 1950s that there would be new desires for housing and moved to satisfy this desire by building new homes and improving lives and communities in Singapore (see Chapter 17). And it was his vision of how Singaporeans would, along with a taste for better housing, develop new desires for other aspects of a better life, including new shopping and dining choices, that prompted him to develop the first shopping malls in Orchard Road in the early 1970s.

In the last 50 years, Far East Organization's real estate business has expanded to cover the full spectrum of the property market, from homes to corporate housing, hotels and serviced residences, and from shopping malls to offices, medical centres, factories and warehouses. As a vendor of real estate products, we are focused on building innovative and functional spaces, and providing high-quality experiences and value for our customers.

In carrying on our legacy of entrepreneurship, we seek to better the way of life of customers through the spaces we build. We have articulated this commitment in our brand statement of "Inspiring Better Lives", supported by our brand attributes of Trustworthy, Customer-centric and Innovative. Underpinning the organisational culture of innovation is a focus on customers. We challenge ourselves to constantly rethink how we can best create value for our customers through new development concepts and ideas, as well as refinements to products and service improvements, all the time being thoughtful of their needs and aspirations. We are driven to constantly innovating, creating effective use of space and making the living experience of customers all that more comfortable. By delivering on the value promise, we build trust with customers.

Organisational Challenges

As Singapore's largest private property developer, our challenge is to ensure that this integral value of customer centricity is upheld through all levels of the organisation and permeates every element of our business, from our residential property business to our hospitality portfolio of hotels and serviced residences where we serve guests from around the world, and from our retail malls and commercial spaces to the industrial facilities we provide. This means that our leaders must have the mindset to make process changes to facilitate a seamless customer experience.

With globalisation, and in a knowledge-based age where the instant exchange of information is the norm, consumers are becoming increasingly sophisticated, well-travelled and demanding. More choices dictate that businesses adopt new practices to win this generation of buyers over. Singapore is also transforming, taking her place among the top cities of the world and presenting an international marketplace for real estate and real estate products. In turn, this has attracted a new influx of affluent customers and created a new market for us to grow and understand. These global customers are well plugged into world-class lifestyle quality, business and leisure options for which they are prepared to pay international prices. Commensurately, they expect international value, standards, quality and calibre in product and service delivery.

Our challenge is to rise to fulfil and fuel the demand and desires of this new market by delivering the requisite value. We have to respond rapidly and fluidly, to keep pace with the international demand and the products that we are leasing or selling. We need to be much more attuned to the life and living of other global cities and markets so that we can better appreciate the lifestyles and preferences of our customers.

The Journey With the Customer

At Far East Organization, we are concerned with giving the market what it wants and needs. The demands and expectations of our customers drive the organisational actions. The strategies, systems and processes that we have put in place to align our internal behaviours to external customers' needs can be categorised into four key areas.

1. Structure

Our organisational structure is composed by design around the focus of meeting customers' needs and aspirations, and how to create value for customers in terms of new concepts and ideas, and improved services. It is also about creating a comfortable and satisfying experience for our customers in their dealings with Far East Organization.

We are always thinking: what is the consequence of a product that is not conceived well? Not built well? Not delivered well? All these are interlinked and affect the experience of the customer. Therefore, we have taken an integrated organisational approach in the end-to-end process from design conceptualisation at the inception of a development project, through project and construction management, to delivery of the completed property to the home purchaser.

The Product Development unit conceives the product that satisfies the customer's needs and creates emotional aspirations. Its functions include architectural and interior design, building of show flats and developing the emotion, character and entrance experience, the sight, the smell, the service — all that is related to the point of sales. So when customers buy, they enjoy not only the product, but also the whole experience of acquiring a home from Far East Organization. The Project Management unit ensures that the product is built according to our quality and safety standards, and is completed on schedule. Throughout the construction process, the customer is kept updated on the progress of development and when his or her new home can be ready.

The Customer Management unit then ensures that, at the delivery stage, when the customer receives the keys to the apartment, we continue to provide a positive experience with thoughtful services that focus on the customer's needs. We recognise that the experience of receiving the product is actually very important. Therefore, we go the extra mile for our customers by attending to the small details, such as providing lights, crockery and towels, and turning on the water supply and air-conditioner so that the home owners and their family can immediately enjoy a small housewarming when they take over their newly completed apartment.

The other part of this delivery comes from everything being done properly; the customer does not want to worry about defects, or that tiles are not aligned and the pipes not checked. Here, the Quality Management unit of the organisation ensures that there are consistent quality processes in place, giving their colleagues the confidence to deliver the completed units to customers.

2. Product Development

To raise the bar in innovation, Far East Organization recognises that it is crucial to rethink the needs of customers constantly. Over time, we have had to refine the design of living spaces to fit the changing needs and lifestyles of people. Space becomes more of a lifestyle orientation and we have to think how it connects people, how it can be flexible or expandable to serve its functional role.

For example, in the early 1990s, Far East Organization introduced the concept of a separate dry kitchen in addition to the traditional wet kitchen in our landed developments in Kew Drive. In subsequent projects, this idea was then further redefined into a flexible multitasking space in condominiums where one can cook, dine and entertain in a casual, open and interactive setting. In one of our latest developments, Silversea, a 383-unit seafront condominium in the East Coast, one can slide a glass door shut to contain the smells of heavy cooking or leave the door open to turn the kitchen into a space for entertaining and dining. This multiple functionality addresses the efficient use of space.

Other product innovations that have been introduced to cater to customers' evolving lifestyle aspirations include private villas in the organisation's distinctively themed condominiums, which come complete with fully equipped kitchens and private dining rooms offering exclusivity, unique views and an array of facilities.

At the luxury end of the residential market, Far East Organization has introduced the concept of "white plans", which allow customers to customise the layout of their homes. The home owner can choose to carve out three bedrooms, or simply have one big contiguous space flowing through the home. We invite the customer to be involved in crafting his or her own unique living space according to individual preferences. The "white plan" concept is a feature of the organisation's ultra-luxurious Inessence collection of bespoke homes.

3. Learning

The nurturing and development of our organisational talent is key to translating the customer-centric mindset into real, tangible employee actions. Leaders must also be in touch with and understand the marketplace, and anticipate the new class of consumers and buyers in the offing.

We are committed to equipping our people with the skills, knowledge and capacity to compete in the new international marketplace which calls for international standards in the way we deliver our products and services. To this end, we have the Far East Organization Alphabet School, a learning and developmental programme to help employees broaden their international perspective and to prepare themselves to serve an international clientele more effectively. Employees are offered travel grants to experience the world's leading cities through the lenses of Arts, Buildings, Culture and Dining.

Another incentive programme, "Bridging Barriers: Foreign Language Sponsorship", encourages staff to take up foreign languages by subsidising both the cost and rewarding progress on the field. They are called upon should there be a need to meet with an international client.

Structured and targeted overseas study trips are organised for staff to visit product launches, exhibitions and landmarks overseas to learn about product design and quality, as well as to experience centres of excellence in service quality.

Our managers participate in workshops and retreats to emphasise core values, and they are challenged to constantly innovate and to create customer-centric solutions. The organisation's training and development programme includes modules on customer service and service excellence.

We also deploy senior managers as "Mystery Shoppers" to assess the customer service standards and quality of service delivery across the organisation's diverse business operations. They are scheduled to visit our residential sales galleries, retail malls, restaurants, hotels and serviced residences. Besides soliciting important feedback to allow the organisation to make adjustments and enhancements in service delivery and product design, this programme also subtly puts staff in the shoes of the customer and encourages them to think of the most minute elements that impact the customer's experience.

4. Business Process Improvement

The Business Process Improvement Awards is an annual organisation-wide competition that recognises and rewards departments or cross-functional work groups which have implemented the most significant process improvements. This programme spurs our people to continuously look for ways to recast and simplify work processes, shorten transaction times, raise productivity and improve the interfaces with customers, business partners and with each other. In this way, the organisation incentivises customer-centric actions. When we are able to serve our customers better, faster and more effectively, our organisational performance improves.

Outcomes

When the direction is to outperform for customers, to rethink and innovate so that customers' needs are addressed at every touch point, the organisation and its employees have clarity in what they need to do better, and differently, in order to succeed. This unites the organisation and focuses the energy, creativity and passion of its employees towards one single focus: the customer. This, in turn, expands the development and the capacity for new constructive changes as customers' needs evolve, and becomes the strong pulse for the enduring enterprise as it engages in a reinforcing circle of satisfying, and creating, new customer desires.

This understanding, and the ability to deliver on our customers' evolving wants and needs, has enabled Far East Organization to create a new ultra-luxury brand, Inessence, to serve a new customer base of high net-worth individuals from all over the world. The Inessence residence is an entirely new product that will fulfil the highest standards of personalisation, privacy, comfort and elegant luxury.

The market recognition of Far East Organization's development projects is underscored by real estate industry bodies, such as the International Real Estate Federation (FIABCI), which awarded the prestigious *Prix d'Excellence* six times to Far East Organization, a record unmatched by any developer in the world. The award honours distinctive projects that demonstrate excellence in all disciplines of the real estate process, including value creation for end users, maximisation of a site's development potential, architectural and building excellence, and positive impact on the environment.

Our customers have also affirmed their confidence in Far East Organization. The number of repeat buyers, as well as buyers who refer their friends and families to purchase Far East homes, have seen an uptrend, accounting for 9% and 4%, respectively, of all property purchases this year.

As Far East Organization celebrates its 50th anniversary in 2010, it is evolving into not just a developer of physical dwelling units putting a roof over four walls, but an enduring enterprise that is inspired to better lives.

4

Principles of Customer Centricity

Dave Ulrich

In 1981, Sim Wong Hoo founded Creative Technology as a computer repair shop based in Singapore. The firm quickly grew to produce memory boards for Apple II, followed by computer enhanced audio capabilities and sound cards. With their Sound Blaster sound card, Creative was able to offer integrated multimedia services to computer vendors. But, as the market changed and these products were woven into the mother board rather than accessories, Creative had to continue to evolve new products. They tried the CD-ROM market, and were early inventors of digital audio and media players which they dominated until Apple introduced the iPod in 2004. In 2006, they settled a patent law suit allowing Apple to license their technology. Currently, Creative is considering speaker systems, MP3 players, headphones, web cameras, video cameras and accessories as a way to renew growth. In his recent Chairman's Message, Sim Wong Hoo (2009) states:

"I share our vision to create a totally new Creative, with a new product line and a new business model, leveraging on the innovative technologies we have developed over the years which will again see Creative set a major trend in the industry and open up opportunities for all."

Much of Creative's challenge of continued growth is not only to create innovative and technologically advanced products and services, but to make sure that their products delight customers. Merely mastering advanced technology without making sure that the technology serves customers is like getting all dressed up but nowhere to go. Corporate makeovers from the inside-out restructure, reorganise and reallocate work, but unless those corporate makeovers define and meet a set of customer needs, they will eventually fail. The ultimate challenge for Creative and other companies in rapidly evolving industries and markets is to understand three principles of customer centricity and answer three associated questions.

Principle 1: Customer Segmentation — Who are our Targeted Customers?

The basic proposition for any company is that value is defined by the receiver more than the giver. I have had a number of aspiring entrepreneurs come to me with what they consider innovative and unique products or services. My first question is: who is the customer for your idea? Unless and until leaders know and target their key customers, their innovative ideas remain inert. Asian leaders also need to define their key customers by being explicit about whom their targeted customers are:

1. A particular market (e.g., one of the emerging markets in Asia, Africa or Northern Europe)?

2. A demographic (Apple targeted their iPod at young music listeners)?
3. A channel (Apple not only sold their products online, but also aggressively through retail channels)?

To regain momentum, leaders in Creative need to redefine and refocus on their targeted customers. They began 30 years ago with a targeted customer base, but as their customers changed, they had to adapt rapidly. Now that their customer base has evolved, they have to quickly figure out who their new targeted customers are.

Far East Organization's sustained success (see Chapter 3) in the Singapore housing market occurred because they knew who their customers were and they adapted to the changing needs of their customers. When high-end customers demanded higher quality residences, Far East Organization learned how to identify and meet those needs.

Asian leaders need to avoid the traps of relying too much on past and present customers, of trying to be all things to all possible customers, and of not adapting as customers' needs change and evolve. Value is defined primarily by the customer and leaders need to know who those customers are.

Principle 2: Customer Value Proposition — What Do They Want from Us?

Once targeted customers have been identified, leaders need to learn what those customers want. For example, many young buyers of MP3 players want simplicity, elegance of design and music quality. Apple's iPod met this need and they took the share from Creative. Leaders need to regularly and rigorously define the extent to which customers desire one of five common customer value propositions:

1. *Price.* Our customers want the lowest price, best deal, discounts and value for money (e.g., online grocery store Yumtrade Singapore is committed to offer low prices: "we work towards money and time saving for you and your family. We retail online and our operation costs are much lower than physical supermarkets. So, we can offer customers more attractive prices when they come shopping with us.").

2. *Speed.* Our customers want to be the first users, early adopters and able to change rapidly (e.g., the Gilt Groupe, an online retailer of luxury items, sells to those who want to be seen as fashion leaders).

3. *Service.* Our customers want ease of use, convenience, fun, responsiveness and accessibility (e.g., Singapore Airlines consistently wins quality service awards from frequent travellers because they work to meet these passengers' needs from the beginning to the end of their journey).

4. *Quality.* Our customers want reliability and predictability, cool design and consistent performance (e.g., the Far East Organization has worked to maintain their reputation as the quality leader in the construction industry).

5. *Innovation.* Our customers want the best design, style, fashion, cutting edge and freshest product or service (e.g., Creative is investing heavily in R&D to maintain their technological advantage).

Leaders may use these five value propositions in a number of ways. First, they may prioritise which of the five value propositions they sense are more important to their customers. We have often asked each member of an executive team to divide 100 points across the five customer value propositions to assess the extent to which there is a shared view of customer expectations. Second, we have asked targeted customers to do likewise and compared the executive team's answers with the targeted customers. The results sometimes showed a mismatch; the executive team may believe in one set of customer expectations that the customers may not share. Third, we have encouraged executives to pick one or two of the five propositions where they want to excel and lead the industry, then to accept parity or industry average in the others. Dividing 100 points equally would likely mean that the organisation is good at many things and great at none. In this case, good is the enemy of great.

Principle 3: Customer-focused Organisation — How Do We Align our Internal Processes to Gain Customer Centricity?

Ultimately, customer centricity requires building relationships with key customers. We have defined four levels of customer relationships, each more complex but creating more value:

1. *Transaction.* We simply meet the customer needs: we are efficient.
2. *Service.* We listen to customers and try to respond to them: we are service-oriented.
3. *Partner.* We work with our customers to identify solutions to their problems: we are partners.
4. *Anticipation.* We anticipate where customers will be and try to help them get there: we are innovators.

)re an organisation moves from transaction to anticipation, the more value it creates for both the customer and
the organisation. Singapore Airlines anticipates that frequent
travellers will not only have to fly, but travel to and from the
airport. They offer their most frequent fliers a car service to
go to and from the airport, thus anticipating a need that may
have gone unexpressed.

We have found that there are six management actions
that can be aligned with external customer expectations. The
more these six actions connect to the customers, the more the
organisation will be able to anticipate the customers' needs.

1. Strategy

One company had drafted a mission and vision statement
along with strategies that would turn aspirations into actions.
They then numbered each copy of this document and those
who read it had to sign in and sign out their copy. Strategies
are not like a sports playbook that you do not want others
to see; they are something that can and should be widely
shared, discussed and debated so that the final strategy
statements (mission, vision or strategies) not only reflect
customers' expectations, but are also understood and acted
on by employees.

One firm had frontline employees surveyed current and
potential customers to find out what they wanted more of and
less of. By engaging employees in customer conversations and
combining those insights into strategic directions, employees
felt immediate commitment to customers they interviewed and
connected to the strategy that meets customers' expectations.
Strategic co-creation takes place when companies and
customers work together to establish a shared direction.

2. Product

Clayton Christensen (2003), a thought leader in R&D, claimed that the root cause of the 75% failure rate of new products was the flawed way marketeers engaged with customers. Too often, new products are designed from the inside-out, not outside-in. Only when we understand the customer's point of view and how the customer experiences the product and market, then can we be more successful more of the time. Having customers co-create innovation comes by living with them and knowing what they need even before they ask for it.

3. Technology

When Wal-Mart sells a product in China, the sale is immediately tracked by the supplier anywhere in the world. Some have said that Wal-Mart is essentially a computer inventory system that connects suppliers and customers. Technology allows immediate tracking of the products sold, more detailed analysis of customer buying patterns (e.g., those who buy product A are also more likely to buy product B), immediate customer feedback (automated customer surveys and tracking) and forums for customer dialogues (social media and blogs).

4. HR Practices

Traditionally, HR practices are designed from the inside-out to meet employees' needs. When these practices are framed and driven by customers' expectations, they have more sustainable impact and bond employees and customers.

For example,

1. In staffing, customers may help define what skills employees should have and participate in sourcing and screening candidates.
2. In training, customers may be participants in the programmes, help deliver the training or be live case studies and examples in the training.
3. In performance management, customers may help define the behaviours and outcomes employees are accountable for and participate in the assessment of progress to determine if employees meet these standards.
4. In communication, customers may help share their experiences with the company's products and services.

As HR practices are defined and delivered from the outside-in, employees and customers are more connected.

5. Culture/Values

Often, culture is defined as the values, norms, attitude and behaviours of those inside the company. Value statements exist in almost every company, but we have found that a sustainable culture begins by identifying what the organisation wants to be known for by its best customers. This means that its culture is essentially the firm's brand that communicates expectations to customers and shapes the actions of its employees.

6. Leadership

In our work on leadership as a brand, we have defined the competencies of leaders through the expectations of customers. When a leadership competency model captures the behaviours associated with the organisation's brand or identity, leaders focus on doing the right things.

The more leaders use these six levers, the more they will be able to anticipate customer expectations and build long-term commitment with them.

Conclusion

All companies must rely on customers, but leaders must focus on targeted customers, understand what they value most and align internal organisation practices to those customers' needs. If Sim Wong Hoo follows these three principles, he will be more able to renew Creative and make sure that its internal innovations align with customers' expectations.

References

Christensen, C. and M. Raynor. (2003). *The Innovator's Solution: Creating and Sustaining Successful Growth*. Boston: Howard Business School Press.

Sim, W.H. (2009). Chairman's message. *Annual Report 2009*. Singapore: Creative Technology.

Yumtrade. *About Us*. http://www.yumtrade.com/aboutus.asp. Accessed on 15 July 2010.

5

The Path to Empowered Empathy

Robert Sutton

T here are still too many companies that pay lip service
to the importance of customers. In reality, they are
indifferent, or even downright hostile, towards those who
use their products or services. Despite claims that "the
customer is the boss", their behaviour towards customers
is reminiscent of American comedian Lily Tomlin's famous
television skit during the final years of American Telephone
and Telegraph's monopoly over phone service in the United
States. Tomlin played a telephone switchboard operator who,
after treating a customer badly, say by hanging up on them,
would happily chirp, "We don't care. We don't have to. We
are the phone company."

Tomlin's line demonstrates the lowest, most dysfunctional
and destructive level of customer service that an
organisational culture can reach: indifference punctuated
by episodes of open contempt. This level of contempt
has become increasingly rare in companies because the

competitive environment would not allow it. Most companies at least reach an intermediate level, one I would call "caring compliance", where employees are trained, rewarded (and sometimes published), measured and monitored to assure that all, or nearly all, customers have an at least acceptable experience according to some established guidelines. A bank might say that all customers should be served within five minutes of walking in the door, a consulting firm might say that all questions from clients should be answered within 24 hours, or a retail chain might insist — as 7-Eleven did years ago when my colleagues and I studied customer service there — that all customers receive greetings, smiles, eye contact and thanks from its customer service staff (Sutton and Rafaeli, 1988).

The CEOs and Chief Human Resources Officers who attended the two-day Executive Roundtable were all in companies that were committed to achieve more than "caring compliance". They described actions they took to be more attuned to what pleased (and annoyed) customers, to learn more about the expectations that customers held about the products and services their companies produced, to fulfil customers' unmet needs, and there was even discussion of the notion that the customer is not always right — that at times they cannot really tell you what they need and would buy in the future. They also described a host of changes they had made to link what their employees do to better satisfy, delight, retain and have more profitable relationships with clients. These ranged from the consumers who purchased small quantities of Procter & Gamble (P&G) products for small sums of money to the long-term consulting projects completed by IDEO, the renowned innovation firm represented by Richard Kelly who leads the firm's Shanghai office. As I listened to these experiences and read about the two companies featured in this section, DBS bank in Chapter 2 and the Far East Organization in Chapter 3, it became clear that all the companies that attended the Roundtable were working to reach what I see as a higher level of commitment to customer service, which I would call "empowered empathy" for customers.

Empowered empathy means two things. First, employees learn to take the customer's or client's perspective, to learn what it feels like to be them during the experience of buying something from or being served by their company. Second, employees have permission — and are encouraged by their leaders, peers, formal evaluation and reward systems — to customise their responses to clients and customers in response to what they need and want most out of their relationship with the company. Kelly described how its approaches, which were first developed for serving the needs of American and European clients, were evolving as they served clients in Asian countries including China, Japan, Korea and Singapore. As a result of listening to clients from these and other Asian countries, experimenting with different approaches and being empowered by IDEO's senior executives to modify their methods and tools to fit the needs of individual clients, Kelly and his colleagues have been changing their approach. For example, Kelly suggested that although many Asian companies are highly innovative, unlike for most Western companies, part of his job is to give themselves permission to acknowledge, recognise and be proud of their own creativity. He saw much of his job as bolstering their creative confidence and to teach them the fine art of "serious play". All this was possible, he emphasised, because IDEO was entrepreneurial and had so little structure and other constraints that his people were free, or more accurately expected, to customise and invent new design approaches in response to their client's particular needs.

The approach taken by the Far East Organization is more structured, using some methods to assure caring compliance and, increasingly, more methods to provide employees with empowered empathy. An interesting example is their use of a "Mystery Shoppers" programme, where diverse Far East staff from around the company pretend to be real customers and visit residential sales sites, retail malls, hotels and so forth in order to assess the quality of customer service. This programme assures caring compliance, as the feedback provided by these mystery shoppers is used to spot problem areas and improve the service that customers received. Also, by using their own staff as mystery shoppers (rather than employing an outside vendor to make such assessments), a wide range of Far East employees learn what it feels like to be a customer, and this builds empathy. Other programmes used by the Far East Organization build this empathy in more direct ways, notably the training and emphasis given on understanding international clientele, along with heavily subsidised visits to other cities outside of Singapore so they can better understand different cultural standards, cuisines and climates that shape the expectations of international clients.

Empathy for customers also leads employees to develop a deep understanding of the different needs and expectations of different customers, in particular to develop a refined understanding of what different kinds of customers want and are willing to pay for (and what they do not want and is not worth paying for in their eyes).

P&G's success at understanding and exploiting marketing segmentation in China provides an instructive case in point. In laundry detergent, for example, they sell a premium formulation to high-end customers, a modified economy formulation to second-tier customers who would not pay for perfumes and water softeners, and now a basic and very inexpensive detergent that they developed for the rural areas and that is aimed at the segment leader at the bottom of the Chinese market, Diao Pai. These segmented products are coupled with sophisticated marketing campaigns that are customised to appeal to each segment. By doing so, P&G is attempting to link its world-class knowledge of marketing and technological issues associated with consumer products with deep empathy about the needs and sensibilities of a wide range of Chinese customers (Ghemawat and Hout, 2008).

The kind of empathy that the Far East Organization and P&G are developing has the most impact when employees have the permission and authority to apply (and even experiment) what they learn about customers' expectations and needs. As DBS expands to broader markets, now including Singapore, Hong Kong, China, Indonesia, India and Taiwan, not only are executives and employees developing a keen understanding of what it feels like to be one of their customers, and the variations in different cultures, the bank's "can-do" programme is empowering its 14,000 employees to take large and small actions that will please and delight customers.

Indeed, the reason that empathy and empowerment are so powerful is that, when blended together, they enable employees to constantly link what they know to what they do, to keep improving their assumptions about what customers want and need, and to keep enhancing the actions taken on their customers' behalf. No employee can learn the perfect solution for every customer after a few experiences. Customers are just too varied and their needs change over time as expectations are raised by technological breakthroughs and superior, or less expensive, offerings from competitors. Rather, following IDEO's design thinking methodology, curious employees are always looking for ways to gain even more empathy for their customers — learning about their families, the places they live, what annoys and delights them, talking to them about what new products and services they would like and what existing ones they love or despise — and then experimenting with prototypes of products and services that seem logical based on what they have learned (Brown, 2009). Then, based on customers' reactions and lessons from others, such as employees who serve the customers, the prototypes are kept, modified or thrown into the scrap heap of once promising ideas that did not quite work out. There are always failures, setbacks and frustrations, but companies that are committed to such continuous "empathy stretching", experimenting and to constantly implement the latest lessons (and doing so week after week and year after year) have a considerable advantage over their competitors. Indeed, the best employees, leaders and companies have grit. They take a long-term perspective and treat the process of learning about customers and using that information to trump competitors as a marathon rather than a sprint.

References

Brown, T. (2009). *Change by Design: How Design Thinking Transforms Organizations and Inspires Innovation*. New York: HarperCollins.

Ghemawat, P. and T. Hout. (2008). Tomorrow's global giants: not the usual suspects. *Harvard Business Review*, (November):80–8.

Sutton, R.I. and A. Rafaeli. (1988). Untangling the relationship between displayed emotions and organisational sales: the case of convenience stores. *Academy of Management Journal*, 31:461–87.

PART TWO

Implementing Strategy

6

Strategic Execution

Howard Thomas

This essay is drawn from extensive personal experience and background in strategic consulting and leadership development in a wide range of organisations (McGee et al, 2010). From this perspective, strategy is an expression of strategic intent, such as the Far East Organization's intent to inspire better lives and to be the developer of choice or DBS Bank's aspiration to be the Asian bank of choice for the new Asia, stretching the organisation to innovate, leverage resources and develop new skills. It is an architecture, a framework, to develop the distinctive competencies or capabilities of an organisation. Thus, strategy encompasses the formulation and articulation of a strategy, perhaps through a strategic planning process or a strategic analysis, and the associated processes of strategic implementation and execution. Therefore, a good strategy is achieved through understanding not only how to achieve a superior competitive position, but also how to execute and develop that position and the organisation's competitive vision over time. In other words, strategic formulation and implementation must be carefully aligned.

In the execution process, the role of the leader (or the leadership team) is to set clearly and simply the organisation's strategic orientation, identity and intent. A good example is provided by Jack Welch during his 20-year tenure from 1980 to 2000 as CEO of General Electric (GE) in the United States. The statement below clearly frames GE's evolution as a successful, diversified and multibusiness corporation:

> "The first step is for the company to define its destiny in broad but clear terms. You need an overarching message, but simple and understandable."

Welch then expressed this as:

> "To become number one and number two in every market we serve and revolutionise this company to have speed and agility of a small enterprise."

Most importantly, the key emphasis in executing strategy must be to identify the key critical resources (assets) and to build the distinctive core competencies, dynamic capabilities and strategic assets that lead to sustainable competitive advantage. To quote David Teece (2009):

> "Dynamic capabilities enable business leaders to create, deploy, and protect the intangible assets that support superior long-run business performance."

An organisation, according to the resource-based view of the firm popularised by Edith Penrose (1959), can be viewed as a collection of resources which are the drivers of strategy and growth of the firm rather than external factors. Resources are inputs into the firm's operations so as to produce goods and services. A resource, therefore, is a tradable asset that enhances a firm's competitive position through increased customer acceptance or cost reduction. Typical examples include geographic location, patents (e.g., MERCK for cholesterol-reducing drugs), capital investment (e.g., GE's multibusiness investment resources and financial health), research and development and innovation (e.g., IBM in services), a strong brand (e.g., Apple), a strong distribution network (e.g., Coca Cola or McDonald's) or skilled human resources (e.g., P&G's marketing and branding skills). Strategists go further, however, and distinguish capabilities from resources. A capability is the ability to perform a task or activity that involves complex patterns of coordination between people and other resources. Capabilities are essentially non-imitable, intangible, rare and non-tradable, and would include research and development expertise, customer service and high-quality manufacturing. Superior customer service might, in the case of Singapore Airlines for example, be achieved through bundling together effective staff recruitment and training, attention to detail, judicious use of customer information systems (e.g., frequent flier lists) and continuous improvement, thus establishing Singapore Airlines as the premier airline for service and customer satisfaction.

In practice, the terms strategic assets, core competencies and dynamic capabilities are equivalent and are used interchangeably in the literature. Therefore, the term core competencies is used here.

Prahalad and Hamel's (1990) article on the core competence of a corporation has had a significant influence on strategy execution and implementation. Their argument is that strategists should build and mobilise resources which, if unique and distinctive, can bring huge rewards to the organisation. They define core competencies as:

"the collective learning in the organisation, especially how to co-ordinate diverse production skills and integrate multiple streams of technologies…"

For example, Honda's core competence and acknowledged excellence in engine and power trains gives it a clear advantage in car, motorcycle, lawnmower and generator businesses. There are three characteristics of a core competence. Competencies should:

1. Provide potential access to a wide variety of markets.
2. Make a significant contribution to the perceived customer benefits of the end product.
3. Be difficult for competitors to imitate.

Prahalad and Hamel argue that very few organisations are likely to build world leadership in more than five or six competencies. Not knowing what are an organisation's core competencies can create difficulties for strategists. For example, they may outsource a function or operation without realising that they have saved some costs at the expense of losing a core competence. Prahalad and Hamel cite the example of Honda, which would never outsource its manufacturing or design to an outside company, versus Chrysler, which has done so. Honda has preserved its core competence in engine and power trains, while Chrysler has not.

The language of core competence is nevertheless hard to put into practice. However, a simple definition of core competence is "the underlying capability that is the distinguishing characteristic of the organisation." It encompasses the way we do things and how we organise the way we do things. It involves systematically communicating this knowledge in the organisation and building upon it. Examples include GE's competencies in technology and innovation, which allowed it to facilitate the speedy adaptation of medical scanners in lower income markets in Asia and developing countries, and IBM's long sequence of successful technological and product innovations, including the switch from hardware and software to services.

The key elements of the core competence, dynamic capabilities approach are summarised below:

1. A competence is, therefore, a bundle of constituent skills and technologies rather than a discrete skill or technology; a core competence is the integration of a variety of individual skills.

2. A core competence is not an asset in the accounting sense of the word. A factory, distribution channel or brand cannot be a core competence, but an aptitude to manage that factory, channel or brand may constitute a core competence.

3. A core competence must make a disproportionate contribution to customer-perceived value. Thus, the distinction between core and non-core competence rests on a distinction between the relative impacts on customer value.

4. A core competence must also be competitively unique. This means that either a competence is held uniquely by one firm in the competitive set, or that a competence which is ubiquitous across an industry must be held at a superior level in the firm.

5. From the corporate (multibusiness) perspective, a core competence should provide an *entrée* into new markets. A particular competence may be core from the perspective of an individual business, but from

a corporate perspective it will not be core if there is no way of imagining an array of new product markets issuing from it.

Core competence leads directly into issues of resource leverage (for value and profit). Core competencies are hardly ever tangible assets; they reflect intangible, sometimes designed but sometimes informal, managerial processes. As intangibles, it is then not surprising that firms are essentially different from one another. Bringing competitive advantage and core competence together as a competitive strategy in practice, we see how managing the business for value and growth depends on both concepts.

Lessons from the Corporate Presentations at the Roundtable

Although detailed case studies of corporate strategy and its execution have not been developed in this case by the corporate CEOs for understandable confidentiality reasons, it was apparent that there was a real and commonly shared concern about identifying and understanding those core competencies and capability gaps so that they can be better leveraged to sustain competitive distinctiveness and advantage. This was a point made very clearly by the CEO of P&G in Asia. Clearly, the organisations and people differ in the way they see themselves and, therefore, in their understanding of what they might achieve. The key tasks of a strategy analyst are in interpreting the external environment, understanding the dynamics of markets and competition, and understanding the internal dynamics of one's own organisation. Core competencies provide the links to these economic assessments through a clarity of perception about the values and beliefs in the firm (often explicit in the mission statement), through tacit knowledge and understanding (that are possibly unique to the firm), and through flexible routines and recipes that enable non-standard challenges to be understood.

However, there were a number of clear themes about core competencies and capabilities-based competition that emerged in the discussion from all the CEOs present. These are presented as sets of core competencies:

1. *Speed.* The ability to respond quickly to customers, new ideas and technologies (e.g., the adaptation of scanners by GE to local markets).

2. *Imagination, interpretation and brainstorming.* The cognitive ability to interpret and map the competitive environment and customer needs.

3. *Agility and adaptation.* The ability to adapt to a range of changing business environments, particularly the Asian context and its diversity for multinational corporations.

4. *Innovation.* The ability to both combine existing key strategic assets and to generate new ideas.

5. *Leadership, intent and consistency.* The ability to provide an overarching framework that enables highly consistent products to be developed for strong customer satisfaction (this was stressed by Lucas Chow, CEO of MediaCorp).

6. *Strategic human capital.* The ability to attract and retain high-quality managers which is seen as critical for the skill base in Asian markets by all the CEOs present.

7. *Risk-taking.* The ability and confidence to take and manage risks mentioned quite clearly by Piyush Gupta, CEO of DBS Bank.
8. *A global mindset.* The ability to operate in a global context effectively as the firm expands (this was stressed by Philip Ng of the Far East Organization in explaining his company's careful growth in Asia and particularly Hong Kong from a very strong local core base, while GE stressed that Asia has a range of different cultures, countries and markets ranging from newly emerging, such as Vietnam and Indonesia, to the more mature market of Singapore).

Allied to building these core competencies was a strong sense that efforts must be made to develop capability training to "plug" these capability gaps, and to create a range of managers capable of operating both horizontally and vertically in organisations, that is, to create multiskilled, highly capable managers capable of leveraging the resources of organisations in Asian and global markets.

References

McGee, J., H. Thomas and D. Wilson. (2010). *Strategy Analysis and Practice* (3rd edition). London: McGraw-Hill Education.

Teece, D.J. (2009). *Dynamic Capabilities and Strategic Management.* Oxford: Oxford University Press.

Penrose, E. (1959). *The Theory of the Growth of the Firm.* Oxford: Basil Blackwell.

Prahalad, C.K. and G. Hamel. (1990). The core competence of the corporation. *Harvard Business Review*, (May/June):79–91.

Strategic Trends on the Horizon

Dave Ulrich

We often ask participants in our training programmes two questions about a business decision:

1. Do we do the right thing or the wrong thing?
2. Do we do it well or poorly?

Of course, these two questions lead to a two-by-two (see Figure 7.1). We then ask the participants to select which cell they want to be in, which is obviously cell 1 (do the right thing well). We then ask: which cell is the most dangerous to be in? Here, most participants fall prey to saying cell 4 (doing the wrong thing poorly). We disagree. We think that the most dangerous cell is 2 (doing the wrong thing well). In cell 2, business leaders persist in what they do well even when it is the wrong thing to do, with their well-intentioned efforts leading to their firm's demise.

Figure 7.1 Risk of strategy

		Are we doing ...	
		The RIGHT thing	The WRONG thing
Are we doing it ...	Well	1	2
	Poorly	3	4

This exercise relates to business strategy. The right strategic thing to do has changed. It is no longer enough to do a SWOT (strengths, weaknesses, opportunities and threats) assessment and to assess the five forces driving a business. In this essay, I lay out some of the "right" ways leaders should approach strategy and offer thoughts on how they might do them well in an Asian context, culminating in a "right thing" strategic self-assessment (see Figure 7.2).

1. Understand the Business Context in Which You Operate

I am coaching a senior business leader who has operations in many countries around the world. As he visits and makes decisions about business in these countries, he confessed to me, privately, that sometimes he feels somewhat lost not knowing the countries where he operates. He wants and does rely on local leaders to make primary decisions, but he feels a stewardship to informing and monitoring those decisions. In our discussion, we identified six areas that leaders going into a new market should pay attention to called STEPED (see Figure 7.3). Now, as he engages in emerging markets, he has a framework to better understand and talk about issues that might affect his business. As leaders work across Asian settings, they need to be sensitive to the local business conditions that shape how business is done. Work in Indonesia is different from work in Vietnam, China or Malaysia.

Figure 7.2 Assessment of current strategic capability

To what extent ...	1 (Low) to 5 (High)
1. ... do I understand key external trends that will shape my organisation?	
2. ... do I have a clear value proposition for the key stakeholders of my organisation?	
3. ... do I have a clear methodology for developing my corporate growth strategy and portfolio?	
4. ... do I have a customer value proposition for targeted customers?	
5. ... do I have a strategic story that is shared both inside and outside my organisation?	
6. ... do I have consensus on my strategy by employees throughout the company?	
7. ... do I audit and invest in building sustained organisation capabilities?	
8. ... do I have indicators for both processes and outcomes?	
9. ... does my organisation have a thorough and regular risk assessment process?	
10. ... do we have an approach for shaping strategy that considers both content (what our strategy is) and commitment (who is involved in defining strategy)?	
TOTAL	

Figure 7.3 Architecture for monitoring external environmental context: STEPED

Category	Questions to ask (to get a sense of what is happening in a country or geographic region/area)
Social	• What are health patterns (physical, emotional)? • What are family patterns (married, not married, divorced, number of children)? • What are religious trends (heritage, activity)? • What is urban/rural mix and movement? • What is lifestyle (workday, weekends, dominant hobbies)? • What is home ownership (apartment, home)? • What are the social problems (e.g., drugs, crime)? • Who are the heroes or famous people from this area (past and present)? • What is the diet and eating patterns?
Technical	• What are their communication mechanisms (media, television) and how independent are they? • What is the level of technological maturity within the geography (Internet use, computer access)? • What is their use of social media?
Economic	• What is the gross domestic product? Relative to others, how is it doing? • What economic cycle are they in (recession, growth)? • What is unemployment? • What are the leading industries? Companies? • What is the economic gap between the haves and have nots (size of middle class)?
Political	• What is their political history? • How much political stability is there? • How much regulation versus private enterprise exists? (what is the role of government in industry?) • How open (versus repressive) is their government? • What is their political heritage (democracy, socialism, parliament, king or family rule)? • What are the political "hot topics" that exist? • What is the relationship of the military and government? • How much corruption is there in decision making?
Environmental	• What are the environmental issues that people are worried about? • How does the geography participate in global conferences and trends?
Demographic	• What is the average age? • What is the birthrate? • What is the education level (public versus private)? • What is the income level (income disparity)?

Question 1: To what extent do I understand key external trends that will shape my organisation?

2. Serve Multiple Stakeholders

Strategy is about making choices so that organisation resources create value for multiple stakeholders. A successful strategy should result in employee productivity, organisation capability, customer share, investor confidence and/or community reputation. An effective strategy balances across these stakeholders and enables a cause and effect among them. Strategic leaders clearly articulate promises to each stakeholder and offer a line of sight of organisation decisions and stakeholder outcomes. This balanced scorecard enables them to connect their activities to the outcomes they desire. Asian leaders need to continually balance multiple stakeholders, with an increased attention to public officials in state-owned enterprises, investors in privately-owned enterprises, and corporate headquarters in multinational corporations.

Question 2: To what extent do I have a clear value proposition for the key stakeholders of my organisation?

3. Articulate a Corporate Growth Strategy and Portfolio

Corporate strategy focuses on the portfolio of businesses within the corporation. As Asian businesses grow, leaders have to decide how to manage that growth. For example, a company strong in manufacturing could expand its manufacturing competence and manufacture similar products for other settings, or it could backward integrate into R&D and engineering or forward integrate into marketing and sales. Selecting the portfolio strategy is important for growing a business. Expanding too rapidly might lead the organisation beyond its level of competence, but failing to expand may limit growth opportunities.

Question 3:   To what extent do I have a clear methodology for developing my corporate growth strategy and portfolio?

4. Develop Business Success by Focusing on Customers

Once a corporate portfolio has been determined, strategy then emphasises how a business will be successful by identifying and serving customers within a particular business. A customer-centric strategy identifies targeted customers, builds a value proposition for them and organises resources to build customer intimacy. Strategic success is measured by customer share where targeted customers build sustainable connections to the organisation. Asian leaders often measure success from the inside-out by their efficiency and may need to shift to measure their success from the outside-in by their customer centricity.

Question 4:   To what extent do I have a customer value proposition for targeted customers?

5. Create a Strategic Story

In recent years, there has been a debate between strategy as aspiration (mission, vision and values) and strategy as analytics (data, scorecards and metrics). One leadership team had spent months crafting their vision, mission, values, intents, strategies, objectives, goals and outcomes. They put them on one sheet of paper, prepared a DVD to explain them and sent this packet to 55,000 employees worldwide. They anticipated that this mailing would help employees rally around a common aspiration. Instead, it created cynicism and isolated employees from the manager's intentions. Another company prepared their strategy through Powerpoint slides which gave enormous analytic detail about costs, profits and customers. Strategy by Powerpoint often has more data than insight, and more analysis than action.

A new approach is emerging that combines aspirations and analytics into a story. Increasingly, strategy may be seen as a story told about the organisation both inside and out. For example, Old Navy, a division of GAP, has created a persona called Jenny. Jenny is now being used by Old Navy to represent a 29-year-old young mother who is the sweet spot of the chain's target customers aged 25 to 35 years old. Decisions are then framed to the extent that they will cause "Jenny" to buy more products.

Question 5:   *To what extent do I have a strategic story that is shared both inside and outside my organisation?*

6. Build Strategic Unity

A new business leader met with his team for a few times and was curious if they had a shared focus about what they were trying to accomplish. To answer his question, he asked each member of his team to write in 20 words or less the question: "What are we trying to accomplish as a team?" Some team members wondered if this was their vision, mission, purpose, strategy or goals. He said to just answer the question. When they posted their responses, they were all able to discern that they had about 80% consensus on what they hoped to accomplish. They were spending a lot of their time debating the final 20% and were not aware that they had significant agreement on what they were trying to do. This simple exercise exposes strategic unity, or how much consensus there is about an organisation's strategy. Leaders, who shape strategy, are as concerned about the consensus about their message as the content. Asian organisations often operate through harmony which needs to include strategic unity.

Question 6:   To what extent do I have consensus on my strategy by employees throughout the company?

7. Align Strategy to Organisation

Strategy has traditionally been a two-step dance: formulation followed by execution. Unfortunately, more strategies have been formulated than executed. To turn strategy into results, we now see strategy as a three-step dance: formulation, capability building and execution. Capability building is the process of shaping an organisation's identity and what it is good at doing. Discrete management actions may be integrated into a sustainable capability that turns strategic aspirations into long-term success. Asian firms that develop the capabilities (or identity) of speed to market, innovation, customer centricity, efficiency and leadership are more likely to make strategy happen. Leaders who attend to capability building will be more successful than those who merely do strategy drafting.

Question 7:   To what extent do I audit and invest in building sustained organisation capabilities?

8. Track the Strategy Outcomes (Scorecard) and Processes (Dashboard)

We get what we inspect, not expect. It is hard to improve without metrics that are clear, timely, specific and actionable. To be implemented, strategies need a scorecard to determine whether the outcomes of the strategy are being accomplished and a dashboard to monitor the antecedents of desired outcomes. The scorecard outcomes often focus on customer and financial results; the dashboard processes on organisation and HR processes. Through quality and six sigma initiatives, many Asian organisations have good dashboards which track work processes and are building good scorecards which track business outcomes.

Question 8: To what extent do I have indicators for both processes and outcomes?

9. Manage Risks

Inability to manage risks has serious consequences. In the financial services sector, lenders failed to account for the economic risks of uncertain or unknown loans and financial derivatives. In the oil industry, the controls for leakage were mismanaged and the oil leak in the Gulf of Mexico ensued. Many leaders today are doing comprehensive risk audits of strategic, operational, financial, compliance and organisational risks. These audits anticipate the potential downsides of leadership decisions and help leaders prepare for what might happen. While all risks can never be analysed or mitigated, they can be anticipated. Asian companies who consider risk will be more able to respond to changing circumstances.

Question 9: To what extent does my organisation have a thorough and regular risk assessment process?

10. Facilitate How Strategy is Created

One executive in a private sector acknowledged that his approach to strategy was "designed by genius" (meaning his team and him) and "implemented by idiots" (meaning those not on his team). This mindset and approach isolates him from the process for building strategic content and commitment. Strategic content often starts broad with an assessment of business conditions and becomes narrow with a focus on the key priorities. Strategic commitment starts narrow with a small team of individuals working on defining the future and goes broad with a widely held, shared commitment to the strategic goals and actions. Leaders need to facilitate both content (by narrowing) and commitment (by broadening) to effectively facilitate strategy.

Question 10: To what extent do we have an approach for shaping strategy that considers both content (what our strategy is) and commitment (who is involved in defining strategy)?

Conclusion

That's it. Ten emerging views and simple questions that audit the extent to which your strategic thinking and actions are current. These questions are summarised in the strategy audit in Figure 7.2 to help ensure that you do the right thing related to strategy. They are not always easy to do, but they help clarify what the right strategy looks like today.

Small Wins and How Leaders Turn Goals into Reality

Robert Sutton

G reat leaders realise that the success of their organisations depends on developing the right strategy. They are equally aware that having the right strategy is completely useless unless it is implemented completely and well. Indeed, organisational theorists, including Jeffrey Pfeffer from Stanford University and Karl Weick from The University of Michigan, have shown that just having the right strategy (as Jim Collins puts it in *Good to Great* [2001]) or big hairy goals alone provides little, if any, competitive advantage. Deciding to do something changes nothing; it is a leader's job to make sure that intention turns into action.

O'Reilly and Pfeffer (2000) show that most companies that dominate their industries use a strategy that is well known and quite well understood by their competitors. But knowing what to do is usually easier than doing it. For example, Southwest Airlines, which has the most consistent record of profit and growth in the US airline industry over the last 30 years, has applied a low-cost and friendly service strategy that is well understood by competitors, yet they have consistently failed to copy.

General Motors, in the years leading up to its bankruptcy, was chock-full of executives and engineers who understood how Toyota consistently made cars that were of higher quality and cost less to produce, but they still could not implement the changes needed to do so (Pfeffer and Sutton, 2006). Indeed, in my conversations with General Motors executives, they explained they had learned that they could not implement the Toyota production system in their plants as well because of the incentives and cultural differences between American and Japanese employees. A history of labour-management strife also meant that there was far less cooperation and information sharing between and among workers and management at General Motors plants than at Toyota plants.

There are dozens, perhaps hundreds, of skills and tactics that are necessary for turning grand goals and strategies into actions. They ranged from keeping the language and plans as simple as possible, to doing a few things well rather than many things badly, to gaining the support and participation of key constituencies, to having the process led and implemented by people who understand the work people are doing, and involving people who grasp the nuances of local organisational politics, and are adept at navigating the most crucial shalts and shalt nots that pervade the regional or national culture. Yet perhaps the most important overarching skill of all for leaders who implement strategies, and which embraces most others, is the ability to keep the overall strategy or big hairy goals in mind at all times and to instill it into their followers' minds as well, while simultaneously and relentlessly devoting the lion's share of their thoughts, feelings and efforts to identifying and implementing *the details* of what must be accomplished day after day. Doing many, many little things, and doing most of them well, is the only way to make the biggest of dreams come true.

Chapter 16 summarises this perspective perfectly and applies the logic to a big goal — changing an organisation's culture:

> "There is a Chinese saying that the journey of a thousand miles begins with a single step. Building organisational culture is much like that; it is an ongoing initiative that needs to be walked out, and not just talked about. In changing behaviours, there are simply no shortcuts or silver bullets."

As Weick (1984) argues in his classic article *Small Wins*, focusing too much attention on large and difficult goals can actually undermine people's ability to achieve those ambitious ends. Weick shows that when people focus their full attention on a difficult task or a big and ambitious goal, it often seems as if it is insurmountable and any little thing they do is so trivial in comparison to the goal that it is hardly worth the trouble. As a result, people are prone to freak out, freeze up and lose hope and motivation. The best leaders counter this tendency with what Weick calls a "small wins strategy", where seemingly overwhelming goals and strategies are broken into bite-size pieces. Doing so comforts people and provides them with concrete guidance. It enables them to make progress towards their goals day after day, which bolsters their confidence and enables them to eventually implement the organisational strategy or to achieve other potentially overwhelming goals.

e CEO I know used a "small wins strategy" at a kick-off meeting for a big sales campaign. Everyone on his senior team know that the goal was to increase sales by at least 20% over the prior years. The strategy for accomplishing this hinged largely on increasing sales among once loyal and lucrative customers who felt that the company's product and associated services had slipped in recent years. At the start of the meeting, several members of the team expressed concerns that the goal was too tough and they would never win back those customers. They were especially worried that so much work needed to be done and they had so little time; some were certain that they were setting themselves up for a visible, embarrassing and financially disastrous failure. Rather than talking about the goals or strategy directly, the CEO responded to this angst by launching a discussion of the actions required to make the campaign a big success. The result was a "to do" list with well over 100 tasks, which led people to worry even more that accomplishing it all in a few months felt impossible. This boss reduced the group's worries by asking them to sort the list into "hard" and "easy" tasks. For each easy task, he asked who could do it and when they could get it done. The group soon realised that they could accomplish over half the tasks pretty quickly. Over the next few days, one small win after another was ticked off the list, optimistic emails flew back and forth among team members touting their accomplishments, and over half of the chores were completed within a week. This pile of early small wins lowered their anxiety, set the stage for more quick wins as they tackled the more difficult tasks, and gave them confidence about the entire campaign. And the group easily met their goal.

A "small wins strategy" can also be seen in the success that GE Healthcare now enjoys in Asia, where it has great success in designing, manufacturing and selling medical equipment such as its high-end Proteus Radiology System. Key parts of their strategy may sound obvious to people who know the region, such as developing much of the software in India and doing much of the manufacturing in China. But the success rests on hundreds of small wins that have been built up over the years, and on overcoming many setbacks too. Khanna (2007) writes that it took GE nearly 20 years to figure out just the right balance of efforts between India and China: how to design a team structure that enables cooperation and information sharing between units in the two countries; how to set up groups that are in competition with each other to spur them to do efficient and effective work (which is consistent with GE's competitive culture); how to bring costs down enough to ensure success in these low-income markets; and how to take steps in both China and India to develop a reputation as a good corporate citizen in both countries (such as the establishment of cutting edge research centres in Bangalore and Shanghai). Yes, there are broad strategies here, such as focusing on software development in India and manufacturing in China and being a good corporate citizen, but the success of these broad strategies would have been impossible without the skill and persistence required to build up thousands and thousands of small wins that were the backbone of implementing these and other strategies.

The power of small wins is especially evident in the success of Singapore Airlines, which has sustained service excellence and cost leadership for over two decades (Heracleous and Wirtz, 2010). The airline has done so, even though achieving enduring success with such a dual strategy is described as impossible by strategy experts, including the renowned Michael Porter. Again, the explanation is in the details: the small wins that Singapore Airlines keeps chalking up and seeking to achieve consistently day after day. As a recent report on the airline explained, "No cost is too small to reduce." Cabin crews are constantly looking for ways to save money without compromising on service; doing everything from taking jam off breakfast trays because most customers did not eat it (but offering it to customers) to keeping their annual champagne costs in the first class cabin down to S$8,000,000 per year by pouring whatever bottle is open — Krug or Dom Perignon — unless the customer specifically requests the other (which reduces costs because less champagne is wasted). Also, the bonus system of Singapore Airlines covers all employees — and individual bonuses can be as high as 50% of base salary in a good year — so all employees have an incentive to cut costs. The emphasis on customer service is just as strong as on cost cutting, with cabin crews receiving four months of training (twice the industry average), which includes schooling in details such as etiquette and cultural sensitivity. For example, flight attendants are taught to interact with Japanese, American and Chinese passengers in different ways. This list just begins to scratch the surface. This dual strategy is evident in thousands of other little, and sometimes big, things that Singapore Airlines does to keep costs low and provide great service.

Another way to think about the "small wins approach" is inspired by the book *Zen in the Art of Archery*, which also shows why it is a mistake to think about big strategies and goals too much (even though they are important). The author, Eugen Herrigel (1971), was a philosopher who visited

Japan in the 1950s to learn archery from a Zen master. He was taught to devote little attention to hitting the target, even though that was what he and his fellow students were trying to accomplish. His Zen master taught them to focus on the pleasures and details of breathing properly, stringing the bow, placing the arrow in the bow, drawing it back and releasing it, though not on hitting the target. By doing so, Herrigel and fellow students "took more pleasure from doing each task and, since they learned to master the nuances (much like the 'small wins strategy'), they hit the target more consistently as well."

As I have suggested elsewhere, the best leaders devote attention to the small steps that they and their people ought to take along the way. Doing so will help them enjoy their work more and increase their odds of success (Sutton, 2010).

References

Collins, J. (2001). *Good to Great: Why Some Companies Make the Leap ... and Others Don't.* New York: HarperCollins.

Heracleous, L. and J. Wirtz. (2010). Singapore Airlines' balancing act. *Harvard Business Review*, (July/August):145–9.

Herrigel, E. (1971). *Zen in the Art of Archery.* New York: Vintage.

Khanna, T. (2007). China + India: the power of two. *Harvard Business Review*, (December):60–9.

O'Reilly III, C.A. and J. Pfeffer. (2000). *Hidden Value.* Boston: Harvard Business School Press.

Pfeffer, J. and R.I. Sutton. (2006). *Hard Facts, Dangerous Half-Truths, and Total Nonsense.* Boston: Harvard Business School Press.

Sutton, R.I. (2010). *Good Boss, Bad Boss.* New York: Business Plus.

Weick, K.E. (1984). Small wins. *American Psychologist*, 39:40–9.

PART THREE

Getting Past the Past

9

Leadership Insights from MediaCorp

Lucas Chow

Introduction

MediaCorp is Singapore's leading media company with the most complete range of platforms spanning television, radio, newspapers, magazines, movies, digital and out-of-home media. It pioneered the development of Singapore's broadcasting industry, with the broadcast of radio in 1936 and television in 1963. Today, MediaCorp has over 50 products and brands in four languages (English, Mandarin, Malay and Tamil) reaching out to all adults in Singapore every week. A winner of numerous international awards and accolades, including Asia Television's Broadcaster of the Year, MediaCorp's vision is to become Asia's top media company delivering valued content to the world.

Today, the challenge for us in MediaCorp is the way all things digital have taken over the world in the past couple of years. From interactive gaming to the iPhone, iPad, high-definition and 3D television, and with such speed and capacity improvement on the national broadband network, it seems technology is coming onstream faster than we can adapt it and adapt to it. As such, the challenge faced by the MediaCorp leadership team is not only to embrace the opportunity of having such a broad base of platforms, but also what technology has to offer to build itself new business areas and models in the digital world. This means managing change in a changing world.

Challenges

Clearly, the set of challenges in transforming is set against a backdrop of an industry that is changing at great speed and a workforce that needs to be skilled and reskilled. In order to build an internal capacity for change to respond to external demands, MediaCorp has focused primarily on two things: defining the mission and staying on course.

Defining the Mission is Critical

This may sound *cliché*, but it is so important and critical for the leader to set forth the basis of where the transformation will move towards. A leader who needs to champion a vision and possess the insights of defining the mission. In our business, where there is convergence of media and telecommunication, we had to reexamine the vision of MediaCorp business. In 2006, my senior management and I reviewed the external situation and environment changes. We were convinced that we need to make a dramatic shift from being just the national broadcaster, especially when we had other business types (non-broadcasting) such as content distribution, documentary and movie production and events businesses. The convergence of telecommunication and media is what I characterised as "5-ons" and "3-screens", that is, on air, on print, online, on demand and on the go, and the deliveries were in the form of the television screen, computer screen and the mobile (phone) screen. This formed the basis when we reexamined our competence in content development and creation, and concluded with the agreement of the senior team to redefine our mission as that of being one "to deliver valued content to the world".

Thus, the clarity of this redefined mission was pervasively cascaded throughout the organisation. Through townhalls and business operations meetings, we communicated that broadcasting is only the delivery platform, but creating content will become the real mission to drive the effectiveness and use of the many platforms Mediacorp has. Since then, this clarity of our mission defined and redefined going forward became the common force that brings all units and platform owners together in MediaCorp, amidst a challenge where the leadership must be prepared to embrace that "none of us is as good as all of us".

As an anecdote, this (re)definition of mission had meant a couple of key changes for us. One of these is radio. Our radio business had been around for almost 75 years. Being a content creator and not just being on air for 13 radio stations, this business had reinvented itself. For example, a radio listener will no longer be just a passive listener. With delivery platforms such as the iPhone, he or she — while listening to a particular song — can now have additional access to information, such as the name of the singer or the song lyrics. The radio experience is now truly different.

Stay on Course: Preparing and Updating a Coherent Strategy

Translating a common mission into common strategies that will achieve our aspiration needs to be built on a leader's ability to articulate the common intent. Engaging at all levels become a critical integration point. Common methodology and language drive connection.

In a given year, I engage with different stakeholders at different times on strategies and update them. I like to engage the senior/middle management team in quarterly meetings to review how we are progressing towards achieving our mission: which areas are we doing well, where are our gaps and barriers, what help do they need, all form part of this dialogue. We also keep a very close eye on competition to drive ourselves and raise our watermark to compete in this challenging industry. It is critical that I make them part of this journey to create that shared ownership. Engaging the workforce is also just as critical. I host roundtable meetings with 12 to 15 employees from a cross-section of the business on a bimonthly basis. This is when many operational barriers are raised and this is where I ensured that all issues, no matter how trivial, are addressed and closed with the participants. These regular roundtables have always served as my sanity check on how we are doing in our journey over the past five years.

My senior management and key business unit leaders review and update key strategies using a common methodology, the Ten-step Hoshin Stategic Planning, every year. The basis for decision making and accountability becomes clear on how each business unit builds its plans. Dealing with facts and information on a common framework is especially effective in our context. Being more fact-based, it gains efficiencies of scale and size while maintaining the intimacy and customisation required by the various types of businesses we have in MediaCorp when using such a common methodology and language.

10

Leading Change at General Electric

Stuart L Dean

General Electric (GE) believes that "when the rate of change inside an institution becomes slower than the rate of change outside, the end is in sight", a belief advocated by Jack Welch that still stands today. GE recognises that "growth" involves change. A leader who wants to grow would need a change of mindset and alignment of behaviours to the desired leadership practices. Change in organisational culture, systems and processes requires stakeholders to change or adapt to new ways of doing things. Growth, in essence, is about "change".

Organisational change at GE is proactively led by the top leadership in GE. What makes GE highly successful in leading and managing change is the ability of its leaders to define, and constantly redefine, the future state the business and people ought to be in to pave the way for success. As Jeffrey Immelt once put it, "A key GE strength is our ability to conceptualize the future, identify the 'unstoppable' trends and develop new ways to grow."

Identifying the future state to show how success would look like allows stakeholders to look at their current state and understand what are the gaps to get to the future state. Building a case for the need to change and putting relevant measurements in place help to track progress of the change process. The culture of change in GE is supported by a whole gamut of systems and processes that are outlined below.

Growth Values

Change requires the ability to see things from different perspectives. To grow "Change Leaders", one of the GE Growth Values is "Imagination and Courage", which aims to direct leaders to think about the need to develop in themselves an innovative mindset and to constantly move beyond the way things are today. It means looking for new ideas, finding the better way and then making it a reality.

GE talent from all over the world are measured on their demonstration of this value. Employees are appraised not only on their work performance, but also on their demonstration of this value and five other Growth Values which are the standards of successful leadership behaviours in GE. The GE Growth Values legitimate a change conversation. It allows employees throughout GE to talk about change without being defensive or backward-looking.

Vision Setting

Vision Setting involves setting standards for the future and making sure people understand what it is and helping them get there through training and strong leadership. One of the strategies leaders at GE use to drive change is to help employees focus on the future, always looking at what lies ahead and needs to be done versus focusing on what was in the past or what was wrong.

In one of the dialogue sessions with university students, Immelt shared how in leading the change he wanted, such as rolling out of the growth traits to build growth leaders, he simply focused on what needed to be done to move the company ahead without making any reference to the past. As people gained momentum to the new practices, old practices were being chipped away progressively without them being conscious of it. This leadership language is especially useful in developing Asian leaders, as people who grew up in the Asian culture tend to be more critical and often articulate what is wrong rather than focusing on what is right or what needs to be done to move forward.

By focusing on the future instead of the past, GE leaders change for what can be more than to move away from what has been. This is important as GE has had a legacy of success and letting go of the past does not invalidate, in any way, the previous success or regimes. But, focusing on the future for change helps GE employees to honour and confirm their past and yet change for their future.

Goal Setting Process

The Goal Setting process also helps employees to focus on what needs to be done to move the company ahead and not stay status quo. It ensures a strong line of sight to the business imperatives and helps to get everybody focused on working on new developments and changes critical to business growth and running in the same direction.

This process starts with Immelt's session with GE's top 600 executives at the Annual Global Leadership Meeting, where he shares the company's strategies and priorities over the next 12 months. The strategies and priorities are framed broadly and allow flexibility for the businesses to translate and adapt to their business environment and local context, but are specific enough to help GE's managers understand which areas require more focus and effort in the coming years, and which will require less than in the past. These are then cascaded to the key businesses and downstream to the different levels of staff to develop individual goals. At the end of the year, each employee is assessed on their performance against a total of up to five goals that are well aligned to the business goals.

With more than 50% of GE's revenue coming from outside of the US, Immelt had — at one of the Annual Global Leadership Meetings — called for the reframing of how we think of globalisation, as connected and scalable localisation. Essentially, this calls for building capabilities, to move forward with an "in country, for country" mindset and hiring the right local talent and empowering them to build their careers in GE.

For example, to connect locally in China, significant investments were made in China, both in terms of people and infrastructure. Amongst others, GE has employed over 12,000 people across the country and has increased the design resources by 20% in Wuxi to create local market products for the rural regions.

In support of the "In China, For China" initiative, GE has also invested heavily in R&D at the Global Research Center in Shanghai to develop advanced, environment friendly technologies such as water purification, low emission aircraft engines and energy efficient power distribution. It has also signed an agreement with Tsinghua University to provide research to GE's ecomagination initiatives in China and around the world.

In India, a region with great potential for growth, GE has shifted its decision making power to India itself and put in more resources locally in terms of more people and more products in-country to realise the growth potential in India. The recent appointment of John Flannery as the President and CEO of GE India to lead the "One GE in India", where all the businesses now report directly to versus to the corporate headquarters outside of India previously, is another example of GE's localisation effort.

GE continues to train, grow and help local talent assimilate into the GE culture, be they in Asia, Europe, the Middle East or Africa, and once they are ready, localised key leadership positions that are held by expatriate leaders. Today, many of the key positions in Asia are held by locals; locals who are trained in the GE operating methods and embrace the GE values, and who have their own unmatchable customer intimacy and market knowledge.

Operating System/Learning Culture

Another key engine of change in GE is the GE Operating System, which is likened to the operating software of the company (see Figure 10.1). It glues the company together with processes and the people. It is GE's learning culture in action, and is an annual integrated business and leadership process that focuses on developing strategies in the core business processes (such as Technology, Compliance, Talent Reviews, Growth Playbook, Operations Plan and Employee Health and Safety) at the global level. It is a year-round series of intense learning sessions where Business CEOs, thought leaders and initiative champions from GE, as well as outside

Figure 10.1 GE Operating System

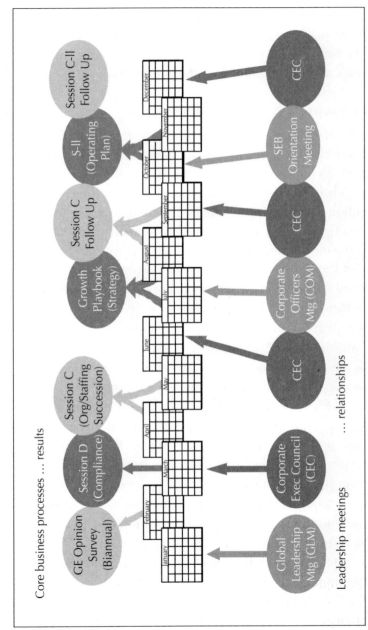

the company, meet and share intellectual capital. The central focus is always on real changes facing the markets/businesses, sharing and putting into action the best ideas and practices from across the company and around the world.

Growing Change Leaders

GE also uses Team Learning at the Senior Leadership level to drive change in its P&L units. This is achieved through the Leadership Innovative and Growth programme, which is sponsored by Immelt. It is a one-week, team-based action learning programme designed to train intact, cross-functional P&L unit leadership teams to help the leaders to connect their strategic vision with the culture, resources and capability of the company. Top senior leaderships are involved in this programme and action plans developed, and leaders are held accountable to deliver in accordance with the plans. P&L units from all regions, including Asia, have participated in these programmes. It is about leading change at the senior leadership level and senior leadership taking ownership of the change needed to grow their business.

GE's strong change culture is the result of its strong senior leadership focus, supported by the rigorous systems and processes it has put in place. Most importantly, GE proactively learns not only from its own leaders, but also from thought leaders, academia and best-in-class companies to constantly challenge the status quo and look out for what the future will look like to sustain business success and working relentlessly to get there.

It is this culture of change and learning that keeps the minds of the GE talent highly engaged, be they in the US, Europe or Asia. Always building a strong case for change and equipping the talent to adapt to the change, and helping them see positive outcomes arising from the change, has helped bridged national boundaries in leading the multicultural workforce.

A Strong Corporate Culture to Support Change

Being a global company, how does GE lead change in different regions with different cultures? While GE has many businesses and employees spanning the globe, it operates like one company. Besides the GE Operating System that ties the processes and people together globally, there is also a distinct corporate culture that unifies GE employees regardless of where they come from.

In an interview with the *Wall Street Journal* in November 2009, John Flannery, President and CEO of GE India, who has spent 22 years in GE and worked across the US, Latin America and Asia, was quoted saying, amongst other things:

> "To a large extent, a strong set of corporate values that is well understood by employees is key to bridging differences across cultures ... Having worked across the US, Latin America and Asia with GE, I find that our people, no matter where they come from, are unified by our distinct corporate culture."

What is this distinct corporate culture? It is the way we work, interact and speak at GE that acts as the unifying force for our businesses and employees around the world. Some of the common leadership practices that are pervasive in GE worldwide are:

1. Value-based leadership behaviours unified through the GE Growth Values and an unyielding integrity
2. Culture of performance and meritocracy

3. Equal opportunity employer with focus on talent development, regardless of the person's race, religion or national origin
4. Sharing culture ... high levels of collaboration
5. Leaders know they are expected to build others
6. We versus me culture
7. High levels of accountability
8. Strong execution
9. Strong learning culture
10. Common leadership language and leadership toolkits

The strong corporate culture helps to support the change process across all countries and reduce the resistance to change due to different country cultures. In countries where GE's presence is new or where there is a need to build the culture, experienced GE leaders are sent to lead the businesses and act as role models. Local leaders are provided exposure to GE's corporate culture with opportunities to visit corporate headquarters, attend Crotonville leadership classes (where participants come from across businesses, across cultures and across countries) and learn from visiting senior leaders who would share their leadership experience and act as role models to support the change process.

Conclusion

Growth is change. In leading change, employees are made to understand how the change initiatives instituted are aimed at growing them as leaders and growing the organisation to compete in the highly competitive market. It is a matter of grow or die; a compelling case for change.

Active leadership involvement and support have been critical in driving successful change in GE. The ability to communicate the future state helps to unify the employees to run in the same direction and have clarity of what they need to change after assessing the current state they are in. Measurement puts in place to measure the progress of the change process provides the discipline and focus for stakeholders to work on the required change.

Change is a journey of renewal with no end in sight. The critical success factors in leading change in GE can be best summed up as follows: strong leadership involvement, learning from the best-in-class, building a compelling case for change, putting in place rigorous systems and processes to support the change efforts, ability to execute, communicate and measure, as well as training and education.

11

Managing Strategic Change

Howard Thomas

The topic of change is ever present in discussions of 21st century organisations (Wilson, 1992). The effects of frequent changes in factors such as global competition, new technology, public policy and regulation provide the backdrop for the change process. Indeed, the topic of navigating change (Hambrick et al, 1998) has generated a set of frameworks for an integrated change agenda involving a series of steps that include understanding organisational purpose, values, strategies, governance, organisational design and structure, operating environment and managerial talent (Kotter, 1996).

Thinking and acting strategically will, of necessity, involve an organisation in some degree of strategic change. Such changes can be to structures, processes, technologies, markets, products and services, ownership and so forth. Change processes themselves can also be characterised, for example, as relatively continuous (that is, piecemeal and evolutionary) or discontinuous (that is, dramatic and revolutionary). It is obviously important to understand the change process, since no matter how sophisticated strategic thinking is, a poorly managed implementation is likely to result in an ineffective strategic change process.

Change is called strategic (rather than operational) when it involves relatively high-level and pervasive changes to the structures, processes and core businesses of the organisation. Such changes are usually novel to the organisation in question (although not necessarily novel in themselves). They are changes which set precedents for subsequent strategic decisions made in the organisation. Once in motion, they are difficult to reverse and tend to be capital hungry (in terms of both human and financial capital).

Continuous change assumes a gradual evolution of changes arising from the current state of affairs in the organisation. Thus, change is incremental, taken in small steps and each change effort continuously builds upon the previous phase of change activity. Strategy implementation is, therefore, concerned with ensuring that current strategies "fit" with existing practice by either not deviating too far from the existing positioning, or adding incrementally to what is already in place. Key examples of this approach can be found in the process improvement approaches of Asian multinational corporations in the automobile manufacturing industries, such as Nissan and Toyota.

Advocates of continuous change emphasise three basic principles:

1. *Continuous improvement.* Individuals in an organisation are dissatisfied with the status quo and constantly strive to do things better. This is the essence of the Kaizen processes advocated by Japanese quality gurus

(e.g., Deming) and the "six sigma" approaches of General Electric (GE).

2. *Continuous learning.* Individuals in an organisation continually update or increase their knowledge base so that the organisation's overall experience base and knowledge management is enhanced.

3. *Constant adaptation to changing conditions.* Organisation design must be flexible so that it is not a barrier to further change.

Some scholars and practitioners, however, argue that change is more often a discontinuous process. This is because organisations are very effective at creating stabilities which act as strong barriers to change. These stabilities can be found in formal and informal systems, standard operating procedures, the distribution of power and the strong ties of organisational culture. They can also be found in factors such as long-term contracts and commitments, fixed investments and inflexible financial and accounting procedures. In addition, at the individual level, reluctance to change and settled ways of doing things render individuals predisposed to maintain the status quo, and to only embark upon change when things become too tough to remain as they are. Groups (social or work) will also exhibit the same behaviours. Organisations will have structural and cultural — institutional — arrangements which act as barriers to change unless significant and threatening events spur action. Industries, too, will exhibit inertia until a crisis point means the equilibrium is punctured and radical change occurs.

A first-rate example of a major discontinuous process of strategic change is provided by Carlos Ghosn (2002), the president and CEO of Nissan (Tokyo), when he describes how he successfully led a turnaround at Nissan, the struggling motor giant, which was causing an atmosphere of crisis for the Nissan-Renault alliance.

Ghosn points out that when he first arrived at the company, established business practices were wreaking huge damage on the company and impeding change. These include financial challenges (cost shortages), as a function of the Japanese Keiretsu system of interlinked suppliers, cultural challenges (such as the promotion by seniority rule in Japan), the lack of incentives for strong job performance and a culture of blame where no individual or part of the company took responsibility for decisions. He made a major organisational change of establishing nine cross-functional teams, including business development, R&D and organisation, to identify and spearhead the radical changes that had to be made. These teams were central to the turnaround. They became a powerful tool for getting the managers to see beyond functional and regional boundaries. He stresses, however, that success in organisational turnaround is not simply a function of organisation change. It requires building trust in the organisation through transparency by nurturing a strong new corporate culture that remained sensitive to Nissan's culture and also built upon the best elements of Japan's national culture.

In summary, this case shows that successful change requires changes in not only systems, but also people, processes and culture.

Change, Individuals and Strategic Leadership

Popular literature (both management and non-management) is replete with the contribution that individuals can make to the success (or otherwise) of the processes and outcomes of change. The example of Carlos Ghosn at Nissan demonstrates how an effective leader created a strong corporate turnaround and change process.

A sizeable proportion of leadership research also examines the contribution of, for example, creative or innovative individuals to drive change in organisations. This has been termed "strategic leadership". It describes how individuals may lead changes in ways which are non-individualistic and are not necessarily related to the charisma or power of the individual concerned. Strategic leadership is concerned with teaching, learning, stewardship and the ability to challenge prevailing modes of thought in the organisation.

Whatever their position in the organisation's hierarchy, strategic leaders are strongly associated with the strategic changes which occur in their organisations. In some cases, this may mean that other individuals (who may be more senior in the hierarchy) defer to these strategic leaders since their abilities or reputation ensures that they have credibility and support. In other cases, strategic leadership may be more systemically anchored. For example, the founders of a family firm, such as the Far East Organization or the owners of a small business, will almost certainly assume a strategic leadership role since they are the "owners" of the business idea and business philosophy. Another way in which strategic leadership may be systemically rooted is through organisational history. For example, an individual chief executive may have implemented very successful strategies in the past, or may have saved the company from decline. Such a history endows this individual with a position of strategic leadership since he/she embodies, or personifies, the organisation, its development and its success. However, some organisations which rely on individual leaders to drive strategic changes have difficulty in sustaining this process through time. In particular, family firms seem to suffer from this lack of continuity.

Just as there are polarised views on whether or not strategy is planned or emerges as a pattern in a stream of decisions, strategic leadership can be viewed from the same, mutually exclusive perspectives. Assuming that strategic leadership is planned means that we view leaders as:

1. Predominantly people who plan a path forward by thinking analytically.
2. Predominantly people who bring past experience to bear on the present situation (the change worked successfully last time, so it should work again in the new situation).
3. Appointable chiefly through their demonstrated analytical ability and foresight, as well as their abilities to think systematically through a problem and come up with an implementation plan.

On the other hand, we may take the position that strategic leadership emerges in organisations rather than it being planned. This perspective means we would view strategic leadership as:

1. Less associated with individuals in key positions, but something which emerges from new and sometimes competing ideas from all parts of the organisation. Capturing such ideas is a key activity and it may be that this is the key role of individual leaders.
2. A role in which highly intuitive individuals who have demonstrated vision should be favoured in any appointment process. These individuals can see what others cannot and are happy to embrace new ways of seeing the organisation or to undertake new ways of working.

The small amount of empirical evidence so far produced on this topic suggests that both approaches can bring performance benefits and can enhance change processes.

Creative Individuals and Change

Once we shift our focus from key "leadership" positions in an organisation, we may see that individuals who have the vision to see beyond the self-evident, and often in quite creative ways, can be the drivers of organisational change wherever they are in the organisational hierarchy. In business organisations, people such as Sloan (General Motors), Carnegie, Packard (Hewlett-Packard) and Barnevik (ABB) are commonly cited as those who questioned received wisdom about organisational designs and manufacturing procedures. They said the unsayable and thought the unthinkable.

In change strategies, the temptation is to seek individuals who have this special insight and foresight. However, they are remarkably rare. As March (1999), the Nobel laureate, reminds us:

> "most current leaders seem to be competent and analytical rather than imaginative and visionary ... they seek to refine the establishment rather than challenge or transform it."

This may be a product of modern times and organisation, or it may simply be that we have learned to distrust creativity alone as a guide for strategic change:

> "The difference between visionary genius and delusional madness is much clearer in history books than in experience." (March, 1999)

Arie de Geus, a noted strategy analyst at Shell, has also pointed out: "You cannot see what your mind has not experienced before."

The problem lies in identifying which novel ideas will turn out to be successful, and which will turn out to be little more than crackpot visions. Note that the capabilities of imagination and creativity were stressed by several CEOs in the seminar, but most notably Lucas Chow of MediaCorp and Richard Kelly of IDEO. The ratio of successful, creative ideas (in practice) to ones which turn out unsuccessful is not good. Most new ideas will not pay off, so we usually retreat into what is knowable, familiar and doable. The paradox here is that without a heavy reliance on conventional thinking, highly creative leadership is in more danger of failing than it is in succeeding.

At the same time, organisations need to have stimuli which encourage new ideas and new ways of thinking and acting strategically. Such leadership (which can come from any part of the organisation, not just senior executives) is commonly termed "transformational" in the management literature. Such leadership seems to centre upon:

1. Successfully coping with and developing the intellectual challenge of new ideas (such as a new or unique competitive position in an evolving environment).

2. Meeting the social and political challenges of keeping dialogue and communication going when different stakeholders view the same world through very different lenses.

3. Having a design in mind which will align the activities, structures and processes in organisations with the strategic intentions. This involves being able to synthesise a great many ideas which may come from all parts of the organisation.

4. Being able to live with the results of the change in terms of both ethics and performance.

Such a list of factors is a tall order. Individuals are notoriously poor in achieving even one of the above factors, never mind all of them. Therefore, the change process needs a continuing focus on three elements:

1. What do leaders do, why are they important and what difference do they create?
2. How can creativity influence strategic change?
3. What is the role of "unbounded" thinking in strategic change?

How can such "unbounded" thinking be fostered? The work by Hamel and Prahalad (1989) offers concepts such as "strategic intent", "strategy as stretch and leverage" and "strategy as revolution". These exhort strategists to set audacious goals and think outside current frames of reference in setting the company's vision. Indeed, Hamel (1994) argues that it is through the activities of revolutionaries and innovators that sustainable competitive strategies are developed.

An example of how an excellent Asian organisation, namely, Singapore Airlines (SIA), promoted "out-of-the-box thinking" was given by former board member of SIA and Chairman of Banyan Tree Holdings, Ho Kwon Ping, at the ISES Global Conference held in the Singapore Management University in July 2010. SIA used a "skunk works" — a young, cross-functional team of potential high fliers — to brainstorm, put forward new ideas and comment upon potential new service innovations.

Lessons from the Corporate Presentations at the Roundtable

There was one dominant theme in the discussion, namely, the characteristics and role of strategic leadership and two secondary themes linking innovation and inspiration to leadership and leading change in competing for the future. Descriptors of the main themes were Leadership in Complexity, Transformational Leadership, Entrepreneurial Leadership, Global Mindset and Leadership, Culture and Leadership and Visionary/Inspirational Leadership.

The corporate leaders also stressed their different contexts and cultures, and the need to align people talent and core capabilities in effectively leading strategic change. This is reinforced by the experiences of Carlos Ghosn at Nissan. As noted in the comments on strategic execution, they also strongly emphasised the importance of training programmes in developing both managerial capability gaps and strategic leadership.

Lessons from the GE Case

An interesting analysis of the GE's approach to leadership in Chapter 10 emphasises many aspects of the integrated change agenda found in the literature on strategy. This is demonstrated particularly in the GE values at the heart of the leadership model, the leadership growth values (the five "growth traits"), the importance of vision and goal setting processes, the GE operating system (the DNA of GE) and the influence of corporate culture in a global context.

The glue that binds the GE leadership model, which embraces constant change across the world, is the common suite of leadership development programmes pioneered and designed at GE's Global Learning Center at Crotonville in New Jersey, but adapted and modified to the needs of regional GE learning centres across the world. This extensive and excellent learning platform ensures that there is a common leadership and global mindset across the world and a sharing of experiences and knowledge management across the organisation. It also reinforces the strong corporate culture existing in GE established under the strategic leadership regimes of both the recent CEOs of GE: Jack Welch and Jeffrey Immelt. For example, Welch developed the GE Corporate University at Crotonville and imbued a new leadership model which has been further enhanced and modified by the influence of Immelt.

GE has not only aligned its strategy to structure, but also to the critical role of leadership and managerial talent in the effective execution of strategy and strategic change. It is still the exemplar and dominant model of how to develop and execute strategy in the multibusiness corporation.

References

Ghosn, C. (2002). Saving the business without losing the company. *Harvard Business Review*, (January):3–11.

Hambrick, D.C., D.A. Nadler and M.L. Tushman. (1998) *Navigating Change*. Boston: Harvard Business School Press.

Hamel, G. and C.K. Prahalad. (1994). *Competing for the Future*. Boston: Harvard Business School Press.

Hamel, G. and C.K. Prahalad. (1989). Strategic intent. *Harvard Business Review*, (May/June):63–76.

Kotter, J.P. (1996). *Leading Change*. Boston: Harvard Business School Press.

March, J.G. (1999). *The Pursuit of Organisational Intelligence*. Oxford: Blackwell.

McGee, J., H. Thomas and D.C. Wilson. (2005). *Strategy: Analysis and Practice*. London: McGraw-Hill.

Wilson, D.C. (1992). *A Strategy of Change*. London: Routledge.

The Challenge of Change in the Asian Context

Debashis Chatterjee

As most businesses worldwide are becoming more and more globalised, the rhetoric of change is heard everywhere. Change and its management seem to have assumed unprecedented significance, especially in Asian businesses, which are aggressively stepping out into the arena of the market economy from the shadowy worlds of government controls and sheltered family business environments.

Change cannot be achieved through thinking about change. Asia is changing not just faster than we think, but it is changing faster than what we *can* think. We have to use another human capacity to grasp the change velocity in our part of the world: the capacity for imagination.

As a tool for change, imagination is one of the core values of multinational corporations (MNCs) such as General Electric (GE), which has a huge presence in Asia. In the words of its CEO, Jeffrey Immelt, imagination is the "ability to conceptualize the future, identify the unstoppable trends and develop new ways to grow." Very few organisations in Asia go beyond the usual analytical thought processes and plans that merely predict the future. Indeed, very few organisations create the future through the bold brushstrokes of imagination. In India, GE's biogas engines are turning cow manure into clean, renewable source of energy. As the largest supplier of desalination plants, this multinational giant is rising to meet the challenge of change on behalf of one billion people who have no access to clean drinking water. GE's leadership knows that it is not enough to think big. In order to succeed in the new economic order, where all the attention is on Asia, imagination must be practised within the boundaries of ecology, cultural sensitivity and integrity which GE does so well.

Change is ecological, and not ego-logical as most top-down leadership models would have us believe. Singapore-based MediaCorp transformed its business from being a national broadcaster to that of a content creator. This was a tectonic shift that demanded a whole new way of reimagining the business. In any ecological shift, the sum of the parts is always greater than any one part. The CEO of MediaCorp, Lucas Chow, acknowledges this need for ecological change when he says, "None of us is as good as all of us." When change is prompted by the ego of the leader, it is thrust upon the organisation like the jerky and hurried opening of an umbrella in a crowded street to thwart the sudden prospect of rain. Alternatively, when change becomes ecological, the change process unfolds delicately like the sprouting of a tree.

Ecological change may be slower, but it is much more enduring. Enduring transformation involves whole-pattern shift as in ecology. For instance, when there is a change of season from summer to monsoon in the Indian subcontinent, the entire landscape changes. The dry and dusty plains of India are transformed into a wet, velvet green landscape. Not just the landscape, but new plants and animals come into being with the change of seasons. There is a whole new re-patterning of energy and a spontaneous, organising principle at work in all forms of ecological change.

The Gujarat Cooperative Milk Marketing Federation Ltd (GCMMF) situated in Anand, West India, is an example of ecological transformation. Known by its popular brand "Amul", the GCMMF has started the White Revolution that has made India the largest producer of milk and dairy products in the world. The salient features of the GCMMF are as follows:

1. A set of village cooperatives that commit themselves to the collective membership of a union of cooperatives.

2. The cooperatives select, from amongst themselves, a team of leaders whom they trust will protect the interests of its members.

3. The cooperatives own facilities such as dairy plants; farmers can hire professionals such as managers, technologists and veterinarians through these cooperatives.

4. The institutional structure serves as an instrument to bring modern technology to the poorest farmers.

5. Because these institutions are directed and controlled by the chosen representatives of the villagers who own them, each farmer participates in the technical and socio-economic changes being brought about.

6. These institutions have evolved their own value system that determines decision making. For example, a veterinarian who cannot cure animals or who is negligent and careless (and whose actions lead to the death of an animal) is dismissed. Similarly, a producer who conducts a private business in milk "on the side" is ineligible to represent fellow members. There is, therefore, a reciprocal and automatic acceptance of disciplinary norms between the producer and the professional.

Dr V.G. Kurien, who pioneered this cooperative farm movement, was instrumental in creating indigenous institutional structures for technical and socio-economic change in the villages of Gujarat in West India. His leadership philosophy is based on managing change through a synthesis of professional management and folk wisdom:

"I believe our dairy and oilseed cooperatives have shown that when the energy and wisdom of our farmers are linked with professional management, there are no limits to what can be achieved." (Kurien, 1978).

Amul is the largest food brand in India and the world's largest pouched milk brand with a turnover of US$67.11 billion from 2008 to 2009. Currently, unions making up this 64-year-old organisation have 2.8 million producer members with an average milk collection of 10.16 million litres a day from 13,141 Village Dairy Cooperative Societies. The overwhelming success of GCMMF and its growing international presence have demonstrated a simple truth about the effective management of change. The truth is that values-based institutions that evolve from the ecological wisdom of the soil and recognise the right to self-determination of its local people can bring about enduring change. Leading change is about leading people to change at their own discretion. Such leaders recognise that human beings want to change voluntarily and resist change through coercion.

Asian countries, such as South Korea and Singapore, have implemented change processes in their business organisations not by fully aping Western management practices, but by following a process of selective discrimination. In their march towards modernity, these countries have succeeded in unlocking the reservoirs of spontaneous energy in their people. Lee Kuan Yew, the architect of modern Singapore, has commented in a parliamentary speech in 1988:

> "We adopt enough of the West to hoist in their science,
> their technology, their competitiveness. Like the Japanese,
> we should try to remain as much ourselves as we can."

In a human organisation, change takes place on the enduring foundation of human identity. As human beings, we accept change that enhances our sense of well-being and identity. Any change that threatens our identity is resisted. That is the law of human nature. Keeping this hypothesis in mind, I offer the following ten principles in the management of change that Asian leaders may find helpful:

1. Any change process based mainly on techno-economic considerations to the neglect of human values is likely to disrupt interpersonal and intrapersonal relationships within the organisation. Such a change will be unsustainable.

2. Management of change must not only ensure that the basic harmony between human beings is undisturbed, but also that the equilibrium between

human beings and their larger society and the environment is maintained.

3. Resistance to change is not necessarily an evil that must be done away with. It has to be seen empathetically as a defence mechanism in humans, which is to resist anything that threatens its identity and ecology.

4. Management of change should not only concern itself with changes in the behaviour, skills and attitudes of people, but should also seek to bring about a more fundamental, values-based transformation in the people. This transformation includes both forward-looking innovation and retrospective restoration of good ideas from the past.

5. The basis for effecting change should not only be objective information, data and facts, but should also include the subjective domain of wisdom that springs from the culture of the soil.

6. Management of change necessitates a holistic and integrated approach to the problems of the organisation, which is conceived as an extension of larger communities such as society and country, and cannot succeed only with the adoption of isolated technical innovations.

7. Innovation of structure and technology must be preceded by alteration and enrichment of the human consciousness. To change or not to change — that is a far more decisive question than the question of how to change.

8. Organisational values expressing beliefs, practices and codes of conduct can be traced to underlying and often unconscious human values, which are

culture-specific. They express a deeper reality and a purpose for existence for the organisation and its members. Management of change must rediscover, sift through and recreate the deeper patterns of reality that exist beyond the structure of the organisation and its immediate context.

9. An act of change creates a subtle tension between the existing order and the potential order that lies in the future. A leader who has to manage change must counter this tension and consciously channel it towards greater harmony and, consequently, greater organisational effectiveness.

10. In this sense, leaders who are change agents must operate from a state of consciousness that makes it possible to undergo self-transformation and self-renewal before they bring about real change in others. To take you back to what Gandhi once said, "I must first be the change I wish to see in my world." (Fischer, 1962)

References

Fischer, L. (Ed.). (1962). *The Essential Gandhi: An Anthology of His Writings on His Life, Work, and Ideas*. New York: Vintage Books.

PART FOUR

Governing Through Decision Making

13

The MediaCorp Story

Lucas Chow

Leading and "Governing" a Team Through Successful Implementation

MediaCorp is Singapore's leading media company with the most complete range of platforms spanning television, radio, newspapers, magazines, movies, digital and out-of-home media. Managing such a diverse organisation will require proper governance as a form of discipline, a form of "law and order" and a form of "culture norms" to guide decision making. Organisationally, it means the expectation of right versus wrong behaviour is consistent throughout — from the top of the organisation to the shop floor. Good and sustainable organisations must have a set of such culture norms and governance to support its mission and vision built on a set of values. In MediaCorp, I seek to drive just that. Good governance is critical for MediaCorp to achieve its mission and vision.

People Management Principles

An effective governance model and management system is key to driving a vision and mission with clarity and purpose. Given the evolution of MediaCorp from a statutory board to a private organisation driving for commercial returns, it is important that my leadership team and I build long-lasting and sustainable changes that are grounded on a set of key people management principles.

Together with the senior management team, we put together a set of seven people management principles that have guided many of our people programmes and consistently drive management behaviour in managing our employees:

1. We recognise that employees are the most important asset.
2. We treat employees fairly and with respect.
3. We foster an environment of open communication and trust.
4. We are an equal opportunity employer and embrace a diverse workforce.
5. Our employees own their career growth and development. We are their facilitators and coaches.
6. We recognise and reward performance with competitive practices and policies.
7. We embrace work-life integration.

At the time of writing, we have embarked on a two-year training programme for 400 people managers and 2,300 individual contributors. So far, 2,800 training days have been accomplished with another 2,300 days to go. There is no easy path to build sustainable organisation capability and we have set a realistic time frame to achieve this shift in the DNA of our workforce and management. Elements of these training programmes include the people management principles as a key to drive common understanding and expectation, performance management and career development and advancement. My intent is to level everyone's understanding and to nurture a culture that will sustain and future proof MediaCorp. We aspire to one day be the preferred employer of choice.

I wrote earlier (see Chapter 9) about how the people management principles can guide our management behaviour and response. During the economic downturn in 2008, MediaCorp was faced with a tough advertising business. Employees are our most important asset (not just important asset). We stuck to the ground to save jobs and implemented unpaid leave of absence throughout the organisation. Now affectionately referred to as MediaCorp Day Offs (MDOs), it is a turning point for the MediaCorp team. My senior management team and I were given the opportunity to turn a difficult business decision to one that increased the level of trust by a quantum leap across the organisation.

Communicating Intent

With a workforce of 2,700 employees and offering flexible working hours, communication is a challenge in MediaCorp. I am a firm believer of how we can send symbolic messages. In the past, when the company achieves quarterly targets I will announce Ice Cream Days. The entire workforce, including all complementary staff and freelancers, will enjoy an ice cream together. This is a simple idea, but it certainly enables many workgroups and their leaders to come together to enjoy a few moments of personal connection. Ice cream is best eaten at the workplace and cannot be enjoyed at a later time. For this, I have often been teased as the "Ice Cream CEO".

Consolidating Silos

I was presented with a challenge to turn a company with divisions that had been operating at arms' length for a long time into one that is run as a "whole". Finding areas where the consolidation of similar work process and business objectives can yield positive gains was something I stepped up to do. Again, the fall back was always to align with our mission to be a content creator. Today, three such business groups have been restructured: the Content Distribution team, NewsHub and the Interactive Media Division. There was never a moment of doubt that we are in the business of content creation; all three groups became the hallmark of our recent organisation development. Bringing together diverse teams that had been distributing content using different platforms, gathering news for different media such as television, radio and online, or even the different "touch and feel" of our more than 50 online portals, I am pleased that this "insistence" on adhering to a coherent strategy has yielded positive business results: increased growth and reduction in redundant expenses.

Future Proofing

The leadership challenge is embedded in future proofing, not only in continuously finding the right business model, but also in continuously building MediaCorp's infrastructure, technology and practices to sustain success. The right leadership capacities will propel business growth and enable a workforce that grows with the business. I am still very excited about the leadership journey which I have embarked on five years ago with MediaCorp, and the media industry continues to provide new opportunities that will challenge my leadership capability beyond its status quo to "get past the past" and "into the future".

14

Linking Decisions, Knowledge and Philosophies to Organisational Action

Robert Sutton

The difference between the right decision and the wrong decision can determine whether an organisation dominates the competition or is crushed by it and, when it comes to issues like employee or consumer safety, this difference can literally have life or death consequences. Yet making great decisions is necessary, but not sufficient, for becoming a great leader or building a great organisation. Despite all the well-deserved hoopla surrounding the process required to make a good one, a decision by itself changes nothing. Deciding to do the right thing is useless unless you actually do it. So a crucial difference between the strongest and the weakest leaders — and between the strongest and the weakest organisations — is that they do not just make good decisions and know the right things to do, but they are also adept at turning such wisdom into organisational action.

I have been studying what leaders and organisations do to turn decisions and knowledge into action for over a

66=

?ba)8lah

decade (Pfeffer and Sutton, 2000, 2006; Sutton, 2010), and thus was struck by the essay that Lucas Chow, the CEO of MediaCorp, contributed to this volume because it touched on so many of the hallmarks of action-oriented leaders and companies. Despite offering over 50 products and brands in four languages, and providing content through multiple avenues including television, radio, newspapers, magazines, films and websites, Mr Chow's essay and his remarks at the Roundtable suggest that this CEO and company make effective use of five especially powerful action tools.

Why, Before, How and What

Our research on the differences between leaders and organisations that have a track record of turning knowledge and decisions into effective action shows that, although they are action-oriented, the rules, procedures and independent actions taken by their members are not just haphazard and disconnected. Rather, there are well-understood philosophies and shared understandings that guide thousands of decisions and actions.

SAS Institute is a privately held software firm that has had impressive profits and had been rated by *Fortune* as one of the best places to work in the US for decades. Its CEO and co-founder, Jim Goodnight's folksy philosophy is that "our most important assets walk out the door every night, and we just hope they come back in the morning." That philosophy propels hundreds of large and small actions that are taken day after day and year after year at SAS to really put employees first, such as providing one of the best employee health plans in the US and world-class onsite childcare (but not onsite care for sick children, because if your child is sick, you as an employee should be home taking care of him or her, not at work). At SAS, they do not just devote lip service to the notion that employees come first.

Similarly, at Amazon.com, CEO Jeff Bezos has been saying, since the founding of the company, that he encourages employees to ask forgiveness later rather than permission in advance. This is because he wants innovative risk-taking and does not want decisions and actions to get bogged down in red tape and political games. To reinforce the message, its most prestigious employee award is called "Just Do It", which is an old pair of Nike shoes because that is Nike's advertising slogan. Employees win it from Bezos for taking actions to help the company and doing so without getting their boss' permission first.

In much the same fashion, I was impressed to see that Mr Chow placed so much emphasis on defining MediaCorp's mission and management principles. I was especially impressed with how, in 2006, Mr Chow and his management team redefined their vision as "to deliver valued content to the world". As he goes on to emphasise, this change in vision meant they are moving from seeing themselves as a national broadcaster to a company that focuses on developing content, and broadcasting as only one platform (albeit, an important one). This vision, as Mr Chow suggests, has helped employees across MediaCorp understand which actions to take and not to take, and also helps them understand that they have a shared mission even though they may be working on very different platforms. A related and equally important philosophy is that "none of us is as good as all of us". These pair of philosophies are not just hollow talk; they have guided extensive changes in MediaCorp's organisational structure where, rather than having diverse and disconnected businesses that operate as independent silos, many business processes have been consolidated and centralised to both save money and to help ensure that cooperative efforts and sharing of content occurs efficiently across groups working on different platforms.

Perhaps the toughest test of a company's philosophy happens during difficult times. MediaCorp demonstrated the power of its people management principles, including recognising people as their most important asset and treating employees with fairness and respect, during the 2008 economic downturn when the company devoted so much energy to saving employees' jobs. The use of "MediaCorp Day Offs" was an especially powerful, tangible and symbolic action. These unpaid leaves of absence not only saved many jobs; the commitment to putting people first went a long way to reinforce the belief throughout the company that fostering an environment of open communication and trust were not just hollow words, but were guidelines that drove leaders' decisions and actions.

Simplicity

Another hallmark of action-oriented leaders is that they make everything as simple as possible. After all, it is hard to implement a decision, philosophy or practice if you cannot understand it. Unfortunately, too many leaders spew out convoluted language ("jargon monoxide" as management guru Polly LaBarre calls it), create incomprehensible plans and invent such complicated procedures that most organisational members have no idea how to get even seemingly simple things done, such as reserving a conference room or getting a raise for their most skilled subordinates, let alone what steps are needed to implement the organisation's strategy.

In contrast, A.G. Lafley served as Procter & Gamble's (P&G) CEO for a decade. He was widely admired for P&G's success during that period, as well as for his wisdom, modesty and persistence. One of his guiding principles was to keep things "Sesame Street simple", that is, to keep language, organisational procedures and plans so simple that you could easily explain them to a five-year-old child. Lafley seemed almost apologetic for many of his catch phrases like "the customer is boss", but such simple principles guided thousands of decisions and actions throughout the company during his tenure as CEO.

I was similarly impressed by the simplicity of the language and ideas advanced by Mr Chow. The mission of delivering valued content certainly qualifies as a simple but powerful idea, as does his previous message in Chapter 9 that "none of us is as good as all of us". Beyond the language, Mr Chow and his team used the power of simplicity to guide both large and small actions. I have already discussed how consolidation of silos was a direct result of MediaCorp's simple philosophies about being a content deliverer and working together cooperatively and efficiently. You can also see the power of simplicity in MediaCorp's Ice Cream Days; the simple human act of taking a little time to enjoy ice cream together when the company achieves quarterly targets creates goodwill and connections among people that ripple throughout the company. When people gently tease Mr Chow for being the "Ice Cream CEO", it brings them together and also further reinforces the company's simple values, including putting people first and treating them with respect. And although differences in pay and responsibility are inevitable and desirable in any organisation, collective experiences that help people see themselves as similar and as connected together are crucial for creating a sense of shared fate and shared mission.

Repetition and Consistency

Action-oriented leaders introduce clarity about which actions to take and when to take them by repeating the same simple ideas again and again, so that people throughout the company receive and believe the same message. As my Stanford colleague Professor Charles O'Reilly tells executives, the wisest leaders can be a bit boring because they say the same things over and over again until everyone understands and internalises them, and they guide what people in the company do and do not do. This was clearly one of the motivations behind the approach taken by MediaCorp when they developed and updated their coherent strategy. The goal, as Mr Chow suggests, was to create conditions where leaders throughout the organisation would use common methods, language and consistently articulate common intent.

Clarity is also enhanced when organisations apply consistent and well-understood methods across units. To that point, MediaCorp's use of the Ten-step Hoshin Strategic Planning process each year means that, although the outcome will vary across its diverse businesses and solutions will be customised to fit the particular business, there will nonetheless be an efficient and well-understood process which allows fact-based decision and actions, and permits learning and useful comparisons across units.

Commitment to Employee Learning and Understanding

Ignorant and badly trained employees cannot effectively turn knowledge into action because they do not know what they should, and should not, be doing. So a hallmark of firms that consistently close the gap between knowing and doing is a commitment to the continuous and effective education of their people through mentoring, norms and rewards that encourage peers to help and guide each other in informal ways, and well-designed and implemented formal training programmes for both newcomers and veteran employees. Doing so is not easy for any company; it requires resources, persistence and the discipline to set aside day-to-day deadlines, demands and pressures, and to act in service of long-term and less vivid goals. As Mr Chow reminds us, there is no easy path to building such sustainable capabilities. But MediaCorp is taking necessary steps by implementing a two-year training programme for 400 managers and 2,300 individual contributors, which is aimed at spreading common values, enabling people throughout the company to understand the common mission and what it means for how they do their particular jobs, and for teaching people work methods, procedures and structures that will help them achieve collective success.

The Attitude of Wisdom

The final hallmark of great leaders and companies is they have what philosophers and psychologists call an "attitude of wisdom", which means they have the courage to act on the best knowledge they have right now, in concert with sufficient humility and self-doubt to change their opinions and actions when better information comes along (Pfeffer and Sutton, 2006). Leaders who have great courage and closed minds are dangerous because they stubbornly cling to failed decisions and actions. In contrast, leaders who lack confidence and are overly humble often lack the courage to act on what they know, and are prone to study and fret over decisions endlessly before acting. When they do act, their insecurities often undermine the follower's confidence, which can damage the implementation of even the best decision.

Mr Chow's closing words about "future proofing" exude the attitude of wisdom. His commitment to continuously finding and implementing the right business model, infrastructure, technologies and people practices suggest he has the confidence and courage to move MediaCorp forward, in concert with the open-mindedness and flexibility to make changes in how the company operates in response to new information and changes in market demands. As Mr Chow suggests, this is the recipe that skilled leaders can use to develop their skills and capabilities so they, and their companies, can "get past the past" and "into the future".

References

Pfeffer, J. and R.I. Sutton. (2000). *The Knowing-Doing Gap*. Boston: Harvard Business School Press.

Pfeffer, J. and R.I. Sutton. (2006). *Hard Facts, Dangerous Half-Truths, and Total Nonsense*. Boston: Harvard Business School Press.

Sutton, R.I. (2010). *Good Boss, Bad Boss*. New York: Business Plus.

The Outcomes and Processes of Good Governance

Dave Ulrich

Culture deals with the implicit patterns, norms and expectations within an organisation. Part of culture is embedded in how leaders govern. At its essence, governance is about how decisions are made. These decisions may be about how the organisation positions itself externally with regulators, customers and communities, and about how leaders manage internally with decisions around strategies, structures and employees.

Governance has become a timely and "hot" topic from boards of directors who have responsibility to oversee management actions to senior leadership teams who shape strategy and define roles throughout a company, to leaders throughout a company whose daily decisions and actions culminate in organisation success, and to employees who respond to and reinforce governance processes.

Governance has also become a challenge of East meets West. I have had similar conversations with friends in different organisations. A Western friend who works in an Eastern-based company is confused and confounded by how his company gets things done. He wonders why things do not happen faster and more clearly. Another friend from Asia in a Western company is equally confused about how her company governs and wonders why impetuous decisions are made and then have to be unmade. They each face the inevitable conflict between how Western and Eastern organisations govern. At the extremes, Table 15.1 captures some of these differences.

The danger of these stereotypes is that they do not reflect good governance in today's more global and ecumenical organisations. Asian leaders who fall prey to only doing things the "Eastern" way will not be able to respond to global pressures. Asian leaders who give in to the "Western" way will lose sight of their heritage and be inattentive to their cultural uniqueness.

In the symposium, everyone recognised that Asian leaders must excel at good governance. We worked to identify how Asian leaders manage the seeming paradoxes between West and East to find a melded governance model which has outcomes, processes and applications.

Governance Outcomes

An Asian (or any) leader needs to make sure that governance efforts lead to important and diverse outcomes. These outcomes require managing the trade-offs between:

Table 15.1 Differences in Western and Eastern approaches to business

Variable	Western: Short Term (Now)	Eastern: Long Term (Future)
Strategy	Leading to allocation of resources today	Leading to positioning the firm for the future
Management philosophy	Management by objectives	Management by shared mindset
Decision making	Fast to decide, longer to sell and implement	Slow to decide, quick to implement
Accountability	Personalised and focused on "I"	Shared and focused on "we"
Work	Linear and focused on the task at hand	Cyclical and focused on the context in which work is done
Career orientation	Generalist	Specialist
Rewards	High pay gap between senior executives and lower employees; pay often based on performance	Lower pay gap between senior executives and lower employees; pay often based on tenure and position
Leadership philosophy	Hands-on, walking ahead of people: "Leadership is done from in front. Never ask others to do what you, if challenged, would not be willing to do yourself." (Xenophon)	Hands-off, walking behind people: "In order to guide people, the leader must put himself behind them. Thus, when he is ahead, they feel no hurt." (Lao Tzu)
Philosophical schools	Christianity	Buddhism, Confucianism, Hinduism, Integral Yoga, Islam, Taoism, Zen

1. *Internal versus external.* Governance outcomes should increase internal employee and organisation results (e.g., employee commitment, organisation innovation), as well as external customer, investor and community confidence.
2. *Short versus long term.* Governance outcomes need to balance immediate results for cash flow and action against plans with longer-term results for innovation and sustainability.
3. *Senior executives versus lower employees.* Good governance creates a sense of commitment from both senior and tenured, and lower and new employees.
4. *Local versus global.* Good governance is measured by good government at both the local level, meeting citizen needs for community services such as education and recreation, and the national level by building infrastructure and political processes to get global leverage.

Asian leaders need to be able to define the outcomes of their organisation's governance process. These outcomes need to be articulated and shared so that leaders and their followers know what governance should produce. These outcomes should show up in a scorecard that leaders can share with others and to which they hold themselves accountable.

Governance Process

To reach the governance outcomes leaders make decisions, both by themselves or through others. Once decisions are made, actions more likely follow. A pattern of decisions shapes an identity. A leader chooses how to spend time, who to spend time with, what information to process, what meetings to hold and what issues come to his or her attention. Through this pattern of decisions, he or she creates a governance process within his or her organisation.

Being clear about decisions and decision protocols enables leaders to intentionally shape good governance. Decision protocols also turn a direction and path into a set of choices. Asian leaders can deliver on the outcomes of governance and meld Eastern and Western approaches by working through five questions.

1. What is the Decision that Needs to be Made?

Often, there are nearly limitless choices for any decision that needs to be made. Simple decisions can get complex very quickly. A decision to open or close a facility may become complex with choices around location, natural resources, human capital availability, regulatory and tax relief, closeness to customers, history and tradition, community support and other political or social implications. To focus decision making, you should not look at endless possibilities, but at the top two or three options.

A senior leader renowned for his ability to execute said that when people met with him, he wanted them to have done their homework so that they could approach him with the options available. In an Asian context, where consensus often builds through dialogue, executives may bring in some Western notion of decision clarity. This does not mean that the Asian leader specifies what the final decision might be (more a Western logic), but lays out options to further the decision process. By laying out options, executives ensure clarity which is a principle of governance.

2. Who is Going to Make the Decision?

Leaders clarify decision rights. The busy leader must focus on the few key decisions he or she personally needs to make. Every decision he or she does not personally need to make gets delegated. Key change decisions may be about people (who to staff an initiative), money (how to fund an initiative), data (how to track an initiative) or accountability (how to follow up on an initiative).

When literally dozens of items seem to require a leader's attention, ask: "What are the two or three decisions you can make, at your level, in the next 30 days?" The answer will likely be clear. If I am not going to make the decision, then who will? Will this decision be made by committee or by a person? Who is ultimately accountable for the decision? What will be the consequences?

Decisions may be made in many ways: majority rule, team consensus, input from others or by a key person alone. Determining decision rights and rules in advance of making decisions clarifies expectations around authority and accountability expectations. When someone expects to have a vote and they only have a voice, they may feel left out. When someone assumes that nothing is done until there is a consensus, they may feel that their point of view was ignored if they did not get their way.

Participation does not mean consensus. Being clear about who makes what decisions builds the governance principles of accountability because if everyone is responsible, no one is accountable, but if one person is accountable, decisions will often be made. Asian leaders may delegate explicitly by publicly assigning someone to make a decision, or they may delegate implicitly by acknowledging the consensus on who is accountable to make a decision.

3. When Will the Decision be Made?

Almost all work will expand to fill the time provided. Deadlines generate commitment to action. As a leader, you can create public deadlines about when decisions will be made.

In one company, once someone was assigned a decision (the above question), they were asked when they would present their recommendation or results. When they specified a specific time and place (in staff meeting in six weeks), the likelihood of decisions being made went up dramatically. In the absence of a deadline, dialogues become debates and debates become endless. The governance principle of timeliness encourages Asian leaders to not only respond to the process of getting work done, but to also be explicit about when the work should be done.

4. How Will We Make a Good Decision?

Making a good decision starts by knowing the quality level the decision requires, as well as the level of acceptance required by others essential to its successful implementation. In terms of quality, does the decision require 99.9% accuracy before deciding (e.g., a matter of personal safety or security) or could a decision be made with 80% accuracy (e.g., a policy that could be adapted over time), but that really needs everyone to be on board before implementing? If quality is the key, the person accountable for the decision must have the knowledge and capability to meet the quality threshold.

Making a good decision based primarily on quality requires involving key people in the process of making the decision. The outcomes of the decision then need to be monitored so that learning can occur. The governance principle of decision quality requires Asian leaders to segment decisions into low versus high risk, and to determine what makes a good decision for each decision category.

5. How Will We Track and Monitor the Decision?

Good governance requires accountability where an individual or team feels responsible for getting something done. This accountability requires standards to know what is expected, data to monitor progress, consequences for missing or meeting goals, and commitment to learning to upgrade future efforts.

Asian leaders have learned, through the quality movement, to have very explicit and transparent metrics that enable continuous improvement. Adapting this methodology, leaders may be clear about desired outcomes from the decision so that learning can occur when results are not fully met.

Summary

As this decision protocol is followed, leaders make decisions that lead to good governance. They not only know what they want, what the options are for getting there and which options work best, but they also have specified the key decisions that will only move the change along and shape sustained governance processes within their organisations.

Governance Applications

Leaders may apply the above decision protocol and governance principles to any number of organisation decisions. In the MediaCorp case, for example, they show how governance applies to managing people. Their case shows how their people-related decisions helped the company to identify and accomplish their goals.

The five governance questions outlined above may also be applied to:

1. *Strategy*, where decisions are made about how to grow the organisation.
2. *Structure*, where decisions are made about how to shape the organisation for the future.
3. *Technology*, with decisions about investing in infrastructure.
4. *Finance*, where decisions are made about investing for profitable growth.

Asian leaders who master these five principles can begin to merge both the Eastern and Western philosophies and govern for results. When they do so, they are more able to deliver the outcomes of good governance.

References

Batra, H. *East versus West Philosophy, Cultural Values and Mindset*. http:// www.thefreelibrary.com/East+versus+West+Philosophy,+Cultural+ Values+and+Mindset+-+by+Hemant...-a01073951527. Accessed on 15 July 2010.

Bibikova, A. and V. Kotelnikov. *East versus West: Philosophy, Cultural Values, and Mindset*. http://www.1000ventures.com/business_ guide/crosscuttings/cultures_east-west-phylosophy.html. Accessed on 15 July 2010

Hofstede, G. (2001). *Culture's Consequences: Comparing Values, Behaviors, Institutions, and Organizations Across Nations*. Los Angeles: Sage Publications.

Hofstede, G., G.J. Hofstede and M. Minkoy. (2010). *Cultures and Organizations: Software for the Mind* (3rd edition). New York: McGraw-Hill.

House R., P.J. Hanges, J. Javidan, P.W. Dorgman and V. Gupta (Eds). (2004). *Culture, Leadership and Organization*. Thousand Oaks, CA: Sage.

Ouchi, W.G. (1981). *Theory Z: How American Business Can Meet the Japanese Challenge*. Reading, MA: Addison-Wesley.

PART FIVE

Inspiring Collective Meaning Making

16

Leadership Through Corporate Social Responsibility

Piyush Gupta

Making Leadership Count

For Hung Eddywing, a surfing holiday in Tioman, Malaysia, turned into a mission to build a basketball court for the children.

In March 2008, Hung, then a vice-president in DBS Bank's technology and operations department in Singapore, was on a surfing vacation in Juara, Tioman. While on holiday, it struck him that there was no sports facility in the entire village. He approached Izan, the owner of the resort he was staying at, with the idea of building a basketball court. She broached it with the village chief, and the headman in turn gathered his community leaders to discuss the matter. The village's leaders liked the idea so much, they identified a prominent site right smack in front of the village's community hall on which the basketball court could be built.

Over the next few weeks, with support from the bank, Hung and three other colleagues had basketball equipment specially manufactured in Singapore. Then, they personally transported the backboard, poles, hoops and 40 pairs of basketball shoes to Juara. They worked with the locals to install the court. When this was completed, they saw the joy on the faces of the children as they played their first game of basketball.

While Hung has since moved with his family to the Gold Coast in Australia, where he now works as an enterprise architect for the local City Council, he still remembers fondly the opportunity provided by the bank to leave a legacy in the lives of the children of Juara. He says:

> "Looking back, we all had great fun visiting the village while giving something back to the community. With appropriate support, and a collective sense of mission and purpose, I am sure most DBS employees would go out of their way to give a hand and help change the world in some way."

Indeed, *FinanceAsia*, a regional financial magazine known for its reportage of the cut and thrust of the world of finance, ran an article in June 2008 on the multitude of creative ways in which DBS staff had fanned out to change the world that year. The article, "Surfing leads to schools: how a DBS banker's holiday turned into a mission to educate children", is emblematic of the leadership, passion and "can-do" spirit we want all our 14,000 employees across the region to exemplify. It also captures the spirit of self-belief and strong culture of empowerment that needs to pervade the entire organisation if DBS is to achieve our ambition of becoming a leading Asian bank.

Building a Culture of "Can-do"

While modern technology has helped to transform the banking sector, the financial services industry is ultimately still a people-driven business.

As DBS makes inroads into a resurgent Asia — the bank has more than 240 branches across our six largest markets, namely, Singapore, Hong Kong, China, Indonesia, India and Taiwan — we need even better access to financial and intellectual capital. Moreover, if people are to be our key differentiator, it is imperative that we build a distinctive DBS culture — one characterised by a strong sense of leadership, ownership and customer centricity across all rungs of the organisation.

There is a Chinese saying that a journey of a thousand miles begins with a single step. Building organisational culture is much like that; it is an ongoing initiative that needs to be walked out, and not just talked about. In changing behaviours, there are simply no shortcuts or silver bullets.

So, how did we set about imbuing this "can-do" spirit in the bank's DNA? By deliberately creating opportunities, both big and small, at work and outside work, for our people to step up to the plate.

Galvanising the Organisation With a Common Vision

One such opportunity we created came in the form of a corporate social responsibility (CSR) initiative we called "Project 40/40".

In 2008, as DBS celebrated our 40th anniversary, we challenged our people to develop 40 community initiatives, to be completed in 40 days, which would impact underprivileged children in the area of learning.

Support from the bank came in the form of small amounts of funding — each approved project received up to S$1,000 — and time out from work (DBS has for years given our employees two days off a year for volunteerism activities). Our senior management also strongly backed the initiative, as the bank believes that children hold the key to Asia's future.

What transpired next floored us. While we expected our people to respond, their enthusiasm surpassed all initial expectations. In fact, midway through the endeavour, the initiative had to be renamed Project 80/40 as the number of projects doubled.

Where the S$1,000 seed funding did not suffice, some of our people happily dug into their own pockets to sponsor the additional costs required to travel to places like Cambodia, East Timor and the Philippines to build libraries, spruce up schools and suchlike.

Another big surprise was the sheer creativity, energy and can-do spirit that we saw unleashed among our people. Banking hours can be notoriously long. Regardless, we had one team of bankers, mostly female, who after work stayed up well past midnight to make handcrafted jewellery for sale (I heard that, at that time, some husbands protested about being victims of neglect but to no avail). This effort raised S$16,000 and paid for school books, warm jackets, educational aids and better furniture for the Bann Huaypong village school in Thailand.

One extremely canny team exploited a loophole in our HR handbook — and the silence on whether it was permissible to wear jeans to work on Fridays — to raise more than S$42,000 for a learning centre in Long Hoa, Vietnam. The idea was a masterstroke for its simplicity. For a donation of S$10, employees who did not have important client meetings could don denim. The team surpassed its fundraising target and irretrievably changed the complexion of dress-down Fridays at DBS.

In China, five colleagues from the Guangdong branch walked nearly two hours to get to a school in Pintian, a mountainous village made inaccessible after being hit by a snowstorm. Whilst there, they delivered food, clothes, books and gifts to 100 students. And in Indonesia, nearly half of our total staff there chipped in to help.

We also witnessed cross-sectional, cross-country community projects. In one initiative, DBS staff from both Singapore and Hong Kong synchronised "skipping a lunch", with proceeds going to a children's charity.

And there is, of course, the basketball court in Juara.

In all, about 1,300 staff across DBS's key markets of Singapore, Hong Kong, Indonesia, India and China signed up to help, touching young lives in 11 countries.

How our CSR Efforts Helped Build Organisational Culture

At DBS, there are a multitude of ways in which we chip in to do our part for the community. For example, as the bank with the largest network, with more than 1,000 ATMs and 600 AXS stations in Singapore, we play a significant role in facilitating public donations towards crisis relief efforts in the region.

In 2008, DBS opened up our self-service banking channels to facilitate donations towards relief efforts in the aftermath of the Sichuan earthquake in China and Cyclone Nargis in Myanmar. Within a month, the public donated about S$3.7 million to the Singapore Red Cross. The bank also donated S$440,000 that year to crisis relief efforts in China and Myanmar.

Last year, we also opened up our self-service banking channels to enable the Singapore public to donate towards earthquake victims in Padang, Indonesia and those affected by Typhoon Ketsana across the region. In addition, amongst other donations, the bank contributed more than S$150,000 to Habitat for Humanity to help rebuild homes in the quake-hit city of Padang, Indonesia.

Beyond these efforts, however, our staff volunteerism activities, typified by initiatives such as Project 80/40, enable us to build organisational culture, stretch our people, foster teamwork and benefit the community. These are some of the positive spin-offs from our CSR volunteerism initiatives:

1. It debunked the misnomer that leadership has to be top-down. The folks who led our Project 80/40 community projects believed in the cause of helping underprivileged children, came up with out-of-the-box ideas and rallied others to execute them. These leaders hailed from across the entire cross-section of the bank, and from all levels of seniority. Our people learnt that they do not have to be bound by hierarchy to lead from the front. A strong sense of purpose, self-belief and fire in the belly is sometimes all it takes to make a difference!

2. It harnessed the collective can-do spirit of our people, and proved that when an entire organisation catches a vision and runs with it, the outcome can be a powerful one — demonstrating, once again, that the whole is greater than the sum of the parts.

3. It fostered a sense of *esprit de corps* within the bank and broke down silos across departments and markets.

A common vision, sometimes outside a formal work setting, can be the glue that is needed to bring people together.

4. It created an environment where ideas could spring forth and where our people were made to feel that their voice could be heard and their actions counted.

Some of these positives have been transported back to the workplace. And so, while the endeavour to build a "can-do" culture within the bank is still very much a work in progress, I would like to think that we have moved the needle in that our people do feel more empowered.

When one of our folks wrote to Izan recently to ask if the basketball court in Juara is still actively used, she replied in the affirmative:

> "Kids and also adults at Juara still use the court; most of the time when I go to Juara town, I can see the kids playing basketball with the adults. I think what you guys did is very good for the kids and the community."

It warms my heart to know that small steps can make a difference.

Building an Enduring Enterprise

Philip Ng

The Challenge: Growing an Entrepreneurial Organisation

Far East Organization was established 50 years ago by our late founding Chairman, Mr Ng Teng Fong. As a young man, Mr Ng had a dream and an ambition to satisfy a nascent desire for new homes among Singaporeans. As the first leader of Far East Organization, his vision was not different from that of the many self-made business people of his time. That vision was to build a business that would endure.

As an Asian family enterprise, Far East Organization holds strongly to values and believes in leaving something of the business behind for future generations. We see ourselves as, simply, stewards of our business. Nothing really belongs to us and our responsibility is to build on what has been entrusted in our care — the Organization's assets, people, processes, products — for the next generation, so that we leave behind a better operation, a better business and a better unit than what we started with.

The leadership challenges facing Far East Organization today concern how we can coalesce a better understanding of the roles and responsibilities of our leaders as stewards. This will then guide us to build on the early vision of our first-generation leader to carry Far East Organization into a new era. We seek to preserve and mobilise the elements of entrepreneurship demonstrated by our founder, which allowed us to grow quickly in the last 50 years to become Singapore's largest private property developer. In this time, we built over 700 developments spanning the full spectrum of the real estate market and 42,000 private homes, or close to one in five private homes, just in Singapore.

Leading With Vision, Reality, Ethics and Courage

Our growth journey at Far East Organization mirrors the Asian family business where there is a strong owner-operator influence. The first-generation founder is the business person and is very hands-on. As we devolve our command-and-control mode to seed greater participation and ownership of our diverse business operations to the stewards of the enterprise, leadership becomes a key imperative. We need to nurture enterprising leaders at all levels who can imbibe the values, philosophy and entrepreneurial energy of the founder and make the transition from an entrepreneur-led to an entrepreneurial organisation.

Here, we at Far East Organization find resonance with philosopher Peter Koestenbaum's premise that the best leaders operate in the four dimensions of Vision, Reality, Ethics and Courage.

Of these four dimensions, we find that much more needs to be done to strengthen the capacity of our leaders in Vision and Reality. Our people generally do not see the big picture as well as our counterparts in other marketplaces, such as Hong Kong. Their sense of business reality is also not as sharp, perhaps due to a lack of international exposure, having operated in a largely domestic market that is rather insulated and where there are some safety nets. These are the challenges which we see confronting us. This is not unique to Far East Organization, as we observe that the same situation applies to a large extent to local corporations in Singapore.

The Journey: Building Infrastructures For a Value-based, Process-oriented and Purpose-driven Culture

The common thread linking the four dimensions of leadership — Vision, Reality, Ethics and Courage — is Truth. Truth in Business is the cornerstone of our value system, which means we emphasise doing business ethically and truthfully. Our purpose is to build a sustainable and durable business, one that is founded on ethical values, strong principles and replicable processes.

For a business to be sustainable, it has to be profitable. Profit is the fuel that sustains growth; there are no two ways about this. Yet, as we go about our business, we place great emphasis on the means and processes. From the Organization's point of view today, the means is much more important than the end. Our aim is to make a profit, but how we make profit is more important than the profit we make.

We believe that if we have the right values and principles, the right processes, products and people in place, the profits will come as a natural outcome. For example, in our property sales operations, we emphasise Truth in Sales. We drum it into our sales people all the time how we want to conduct ourselves and do our business — with integrity and truth. In our product development process, every home is planned carefully to deliver functional and usable space effectively. Features such as balconies, air-conditioner ledges and planter boxes are correctly sized to serve their purpose. Each show flat is built and certified by architects to match the area specifications of the actual unit that will be delivered to the home buyer.

Integrity is central to our core values, BUILD, which denotes Business excellence, Unity, Integrity, Loyalty and Diligence. They guide all aspects of our behaviour to fulfil our mission to be The Developer of Choice. In carrying out our business, we want Far East Organization to evolve, grow and develop in a manner that brings value, not just to the owners of the family enterprise, but also other stakeholders in our ecosystem.

These stakeholders encompass an extended group: our employees who earn their livelihoods by serving the Organization; our business partners — bankers, lawyers, consultants, contractors, realtors and other service partners — who support our projects and facilitate various aspects of our business operations; and our customers — home purchasers, hotel guests, tenants of our corporate housing, serviced residences, business spaces, shopping malls and their shoppers — who consume our products and are the reason we exist.

Inspiring Better Lives

The leaders and stewards of Far East Organization have a responsibility to our stakeholders to ensure that they are beneficiaries of the value that is created by our business and that their lives are bettered. Whether it is in creating private spa alcoves in a sky garden setting for the enjoyment of residents, or a distinctive rooftop dining experience at our Orchard Central shopping mall; whether it is providing opportunities for our tenants to grow their business, or funding our employees to savour the sights and sounds of Paris or Tokyo, we want to be sure that we are doing something that will improve the way of life of people. This sense of purpose goes beyond financial gain and brings meaning to our brand aspiration of "Inspiring Better Lives". To inspire other people's lives, we ourselves need to be inspired first.

Organisational development is intertwined with the personal development of our employees. By emphasising their personal development, and by melding personal and organisational identity, we build a lasting connection between the individuals and the organisation. There is clarity and unity of purpose, and an alignment of the Organization's core values, BUILD, as well as our brand attributes, which are Trustworthy, Innovative and Customer-centric. It is important that our people subscribe to these values in the way we conduct our business and our personal life. Towards this end, we have been nurturing a collegial, sharing culture among our people with numerous communication platforms to connect with various strata of the Organization, along with a diversity of leadership development programmes.

For example, the Chief Executive Officer and senior management hold regular dialogues and workshops with our young managers and executives to share perspectives and imperatives of our diverse businesses, the processes that are needed to sustain robust operations, and breaking down boundaries and uniting with a single-minded focus on serving the marketplace and our end customers well.

Inculcating Customer-centric Actions

Our Product Development team understands that being innovative means being able to respond to the needs and wants of the market and thinking afresh about how we are creating the best value for the customer through the products we develop. The team constantly challenges itself to create new lifestyle concepts with the best mix of facilities, features and finishes to deliver a whole new live-work-and-play experience to our customers. As an example, in Far East Organization's latest mixed-use project, The Greenwich, we have conceptualised a distinctive "trans-urban" development which will transform a well-established, suburban residential enclave into a vibrant, live-work-and-play urban village. The Greenwich comprises residential apartments that include SOHO-type units with distinctive high ceilings and practical, functional spaces which can be designed as efficient home offices, as well as a trendy food and beverage and retail lifestyle mall, Greenwich V. This melding of living, working and leisure spaces brings out The Greenwich's definitive "trans-urban" experience.

Similarly, in other parts of our operations, this customer centricity of our people is at the heart of the Organization's success. Our progress in service standards is evident at our Hospitality division, where our frontline employees were recognised with a record 67 awards in the Excellent Service Award 2009, including a SuperStar Award which was bestowed upon our Senior Guest Services Executive at Orchard Parade Hotel, Candice Ang. In the award citation for Candice, one of the reasons for her winning the coveted award was the special thoughtfulness in the way she helped a guest who was ill and required immediate medical attention. Candice took her to the hospital, gave her care, looked after her, called her family to apprise them of the situation and did many other things that were above and beyond her call of duty. The willingness of our people, like Candice, to go the extra mile and to do more for the Organization and the customer stands us in good stead for the future.

Building the Middle Management: Our Key to Becoming an Entrepreneurial Organisation

A key focus of the leadership development programmes at Far East Organization is to build a strong and effective middle management. We believe that the entrepreneur leader or top management at the apex of a company can build a good organisation and a good brand with a vision, the right values, products and models of operation. However, the translation of this vision — understanding what the business wants to do and how to get to where we want to go — rests on the middle management.

Here, we have identified a need to further develop and strengthen the leadership capacity of our middle managers. They represent Far East Organization in interfacing with our customers, business partners, public sector agencies and other stakeholders. Very often, they are the bridge between the top management and the customers whom we serve. Our own observation of the situation on the ground tells us that there are still instances where our middle managers might not have appreciated fully how to operationalise the business ideas, initiatives and intentions that we have put in place in the Organization.

To address this gap, to help our middle managers understand the business better and to contribute more effectively, we use a simple "ABCD" framework to coalesce an alignment of values and collective purpose towards building Far East Organization into an enterprise that "inspires better lives".

To be an effective leader in Far East Organization, our middle managers need to be:

Aligned	Branded	Committed	Discerning
• Values-based collective thinking • Resonance of philosophy, processes	• Brand as a verb entailing ambassadorial deeds and actions • Brand attributes: trustworthy, innovative, customer-centric	• Time and terms • Long-term vision • Enduring responsibility, truth, honour and respect • Stewardship	• Reasoning and judgement • Precision, clear-sightedness and understanding • Standards setting and expectations

Our Programmes

Far East Organization sets aside an annual commitment of more than S$4 million in training and development for a workforce of some 1,600 employees in our property and hospitality businesses. We have also implemented a diverse range of staff benefits and programmes that nurture and develop employees and help them feel connected to the organisation. These initiatives fulfil various thrusts, which are outlined in Table 17.1 with appropriate examples.

Table 17.1 Initiatives to nurture and develop employees in Far East Organization

Thrust	Programme
Driving business performance, transparency and participation	• Strong focus on performance and business targets to steer staff towards unified organisational goals • Regular sharing of business performance and tracking of actual performance against set targets • Performance-based bonus and incentive plans, as well as performance-driven awards
Developing leaders	• Leadership Speakers Series: our flagship series where external leaders in various fields share their leadership stories with our management staff • Various communication programmes to build business knowledge and understanding, as well as to foster *esprit de corps* in the organisation. Examples include management forums, cross-functional workshops, committee work, hands-on projects, executive learning platforms and interactive grassroots communication sessions • Overseas study trips to broaden exposure
Leveraging core values	• Long Service Awards: awarded to staff in recognition of their loyalty and commitment to the organisation • Outstanding Employee Awards: recognition of employees who demonstrate ambassadorial qualities • Orientation Programme: inducting new recruits into the organisational philosophy, work ethics, operating process and business goals

Allocating non-financial rewards

- Healthy Lifestyle Benefit Award: a substantial cash award to encourage staff to lead and live a healthy lifestyle
- "Spot" Award: to instantly reward staff with good customer service and service attitude, and serves to encourage desirable service behaviours that are in line with the organisation's mission and values
- Special rates for staff to experience stays at our hotels and serviced residences, as well as fully paid dining and shopping experiences, for a better understanding of the organisation's businesses

Personalising the workplace

- Birthday Leave: a day off is granted to staff whose birthday falls on a working day
- Annual Awards Ceremony and Dinner and Dance to celebrate the efforts and contributions made by the staff towards the collective purpose
- Annual Family Day: involving staffs' families and partners in our journey of building an enduring enterprise

A Shared Vision

As Far East Organization enters a new era, our founder and Chairman Mr Ng Teng Fong's vision of an enduring enterprise is more relevant than ever. Today, the Organization is evolving into a truly entrepreneurial, diverse organisation that embraces creativity and operational autonomy. Our businesses have grown in breadth and depth with annual revenues of some S$3 billion from property trading, as well as recurrent income from our investment properties which include shopping malls, hotels, offices, serviced residences, corporate housing, factories and warehouses.

We aim to foster an organisational environment where our leaders and executives down the line challenge themselves with their personal vision, leadership and action. Their empowerment will be activated by a deep understanding of our business imperatives. Towards this end, we have established various Executive Committees at Far East Organization — Branding, Corporate Real Estate Business Group, Food and Beverage, Hospitality and Retail Business Group — to institute a quasi-board process, where the operating management can be guided by experienced independents giving oversight alongside our Top Executives. In this way, our operating management is challenged to achieve set goals while being groomed and developed towards growing our various types of businesses in a sustainable manner.

The outcome is a shared vision, a creative synthesis of our people's individual aspirations as they participate in the business to be the breath and life of Far East Organization, to truly lead our operations and to serve our customers with love. This collective purpose will take our enterprise to a new realm as we turn opportunities into business growth and inspire better lives for all.

Reference

LaBarre, P. (2000). Do you have the will to lead? *Fast Company Magazine*, Issue 32 (March):222.

The Organisation's Search For Meaning

Debashis Chatterjee

M ost organisations in Asia start looking for purpose in the wrong place: inside themselves and in their narrow preoccupation with achieving goals and hitting targets. Leaders of many organisations in Asia that I have researched are struggling to keep up with the breathtaking growth that the Chinese and the Indian economies have engineered in the last decade. These leaders often ask consultants to define what the industry best practices are. Or worse still, they worry about how to quickly copy these best practices from others without really knowing what the purpose of their own business is.

According to Peter Drucker several years ago, there is only one valid definition of business purpose: to create or serve the customer. Drucker was simply emphasising the point that the purpose of any business was to create value that makes sense to and holds some meaning for its potential customers:

"We exist to provide value to our customers, to make their lives better via lower prices and greater selection. All else is secondary."

This is the purpose of the existence of Wal-Mart. Its stated purpose gives the company continuity in time and defines the rationale for its continuing existence. Can you imagine any organisation whose members do not want the continuity of its life? It is the deep-seated life instinct of an organisation that impels its members to search for life-affirming purpose.

For Kumar Mangalam Birla of the Aditya Birla Group, one of India's foremost multinational conglomerate:

"Our philosophy is that we want to be the last man standing. That is, we want to be among the lowest-cost producers in the world so that when the product cycle is down, we are still competitive."

This Group earns US$29 billion of its revenues in the 25 countries that it operates as a low-cost and high-value mining and metals business. Birla argues that there is no substitute for low cost and high productivity, as this would mean an enduring relationship with his customers even during a prolonged recession.

Purpose creates meaning that holds an organisation in a web of inclusion. Take the example of Tata Steel, India's largest private-sector steel manufacturing company based in Jamshedpur, Jharkhand. Founded in 1907, it is now more than 100 years old. Tata Steel describes the purpose of its existence in the following words: "We also make steel." The commercial value of Tata Steel in making profits for its shareholders is seen by the company as a consequence of its embracing a much broader purpose. Its commercial value lies in asset building, while its purpose lies in building an enduring institution. This purpose drives Tata Steel's vision: we aspire to the global steel industry benchmark for value creation and corporate citizenship. Its stated purpose fuels a process of inclusive growth for the organisation. In this, every person contributes to the blueprint of the organisation's future. The fact that a core human purpose is more likely than not to lead to or result in commercial value is established by the continuing success of Tata Steel as one of India's most valuable companies. It is the world's seventh largest steel company today, with an annual crude steel capacity of 31 million tonnes. It is currently ranked 258th on Fortune Global 500.

DBS permeates its purpose with a strong sense of ownership and customer centricity across all rungs of the organisation. What makes its people passionate about giving their valuable time in community development is, in essence, the creative fire that purpose ignites in human beings. What DBS really promotes among its employees is the value of volunteerism by giving seed funding for projects that make a difference to the lives of underprivileged communities. It is the same human value of volunteerism that translates as customer centricity in DBS employees. What ties the employee to the customer is the employee's willingness to volunteer time to listen to the customer from a deeper human perspective. For the employee, it is not that the customer comes first as is commonly stated, but the human being comes first and the customer follows!

Far East Organization describes its purpose as that of building an enduring organisation by inspiring better lives for customer. This is an entrepreneur-led organisation that defines its purpose in terms of the value it proposes to create for its customers (inspiring better lives). The substantial cash award, in the form of Healthy Lifestyle Benefit Award that the company gives to its employees, helps to reinforce the value of "better lives" to an employee, who is more likely than not to transmit this value to a potential customer in the course of a transaction.

A sustainable purpose evokes an organisation's commitment to such universal human values as generosity, service orientation and a genuine empathy towards a customer's needs. Human values are the invisible roots of organisational values. They determine the rationale for which an organisation exists. Human values are distinct from commercial values in that they are not so much guided by the will to get, as they are by the will to give.

Sony wants its employees "to experience the sheer joy that comes from the advancement, application and innovation of technology that benefits the general public." Sony thrives on the will to give its customers joy and happiness. Its will to gain a larger market share for itself is subordinated to the pursuit of larger and higher human values. These same human values connect the organisation to the market and to the potential customer in a network of reciprocity based on trust and goodwill.

The task of a leader in an organisation is to nurture organisational values, which consist of nothing but a basic human aspiration: the will to give. Human values come from our deeper state of being (purpose) where we are not asking, "What is there in it for me?" Rather, in the very depths of our soul, we humans are asking ourselves, "What can I contribute? How can I share myself with others? What can I leave behind for posterity?" Each one of us in an organisation is looking for the freedom to be our ampler self ad for the freedom to serve others to the best of our capacity. Our deepest aspirations are not quite met in wanting more and more for ourselves, but rather in wanting to give more of ourselves to others and to make a difference. A leader is a projection of this common aspiration. A leader stands at the intersection of the larger human, organisation and customer values. This shared space is where the purpose statement of an organisation emanates.

In a survey of 1,000 managers in 12 Indian organisations spread throughout the country, which I conducted for the Indian Institute of Management, my researchers asked: "What are some of the qualities that managers look for in a corporate leader?" The respondents gave the following as the top five attributes of a good leader:

1. Dynamism
2. Inspiring character
3. Vision
4. Ethical values
5. Spiritual strength

It was evident from the responses that Indian managers were defining leadership from the deeper perspective of core spiritual and human values, and not merely as a function of managerial skills. The core leadership values of character, spiritual strength and vision remain the cornerstone of the highest aspirations of managers. The study further revealed a cultural congruence within the Indian tradition that prompted managers from different parts of the country to subscribe to the same set of values despite differences in age, sex, language and qualification.

In a 1993 article in *Time* magazine, James Walsh examined how Confucian societies in Asia, such as those in Singapore and Taiwan, are challenging Western liberalism with their own ideas of democratic values. The Confucian ethos is a legacy inherited from many ancient sages, including Lao Tzu. This ethos emphasises the following human values: communitarian standards, deference to elders and to those in authority, and civic responsibility in place of civil rights. The Confucian values system upholds the tradition of hierarchy and duty implicit in the social structure and psychological bent of most Asian cultures. These cultures demonstrate their deference to the leader, often regarded as sacred, whom Confucius compares with the wind: "The grass must bend when the wind blows over it."

The capacity of leadership in Confucian democracies is determined by a deeply held human value: the ability to bring about harmony in human relationships. Confucianism emphasises the principle of harmony in all aspects of personal, social and organisational relationships. Mencius, an ancient scholar of the Confucian school, spoke of five basic harmonies:

> "... between father and son, there should be affection; between ruler and minister, there should be righteousness; between husband and wife, there should be attention to their separate functions; between old and young, there should be a proper order; and between friends, there should be faithfulness." (Chan, 1963)

In present-day Taiwan, the age-old human value of harmony still serves as the core leadership principle in politics and business. In the words of Yao Chia-Wen, a leader of Taiwan's democratic political party:

> "Harmony is more important in our society, so people do not put so much value on equality or personal freedom." (Walsh, 1993)

We can, therefore, see how purpose is often expressed in terms of human values that fit the cultural contexts in which businesses are embedded. With the modernisation of Asia, the gap between Asian collectivism and Western individualistic value systems appears to be narrowing. What holds true, however, is the deep connection of human purpose with universally held human values such as truth, freedom and love.

Here is a summary of those principles that govern the purpose of a business and how it could drive Asian business on the path of sustainable prosperity:

1. Purpose is not the same as just being successful in achieving goals that the company sets for itself. Goals are transient and self-centred. Purpose is enduring and customer-centred.

2. A vision statement that is laminated on company premises makes no sense until it is illuminated as shared meaning and lived as a collective purpose. To be really alive in an organisation is to live with a purpose.

3. These are the drivers of purpose: human values, organisation, customer and a country's culture. A leader has to be sensitive to all these four dimensions while formulating a purpose statement.

4. Purpose demands an intentional commitment to "giving" rather than "taking". Giving implies focusing on what matters most to the customers rather than what a company can take from them.

5. Purpose implies commitment to core human values. Quite often, Asian businesses demonstrate a commitment to communitarian values, such as harmony and social upliftment, that are culturally

congruent. Most businesses, however, make half-hearted commitment to competing values such as market share versus social responsibility. This invariably leads to mediocre performance in the long run.

6. A purpose needs to be strong enough to hold an organisation even during a downturn. It must ignite passion and include, rather than exclude, a large number of people.

7. Purpose ensures that an organisation's deeds are consistent with its creed.

8. Purpose transcends and includes any role within the organisation. Indeed, purpose is greater than any role as it shapes those social forces that go beyond role boundaries. Thus, purpose inspires shared meaning and ignites hope and affirmation in people. It is this shared meaning that creates real value for customers. Great organisations actually sell "meaning" and "trust" through a product or a service. It is not so much the material value of the product, but the meaning making and trust creating process that generates enduring customers for the organisation.

References

Chan, W-T. (1963). *A Souce Book in Chinese Philosophy*. Princeton: Princeton University Press.

Drucker, P.F. *The Purpose of a Business is to Create a Customer*. http://www.brainyquote.com/quotes/quotes/p/peterdruck154447.html. Accessed on 15 July 2010.

Walsh, J. (1993, June 14). Asia's different drum. *Time*, 16–9.

Collective Purpose

Michael Jenkins

The Principles

C ollective purpose finds expression in the answer to the question: "Fundamentally, why are we here, doing what we are doing?" and helps to give meaning to work. Companies sometimes use the term interchangeably or confuse it with mission and vision. Thus, it is important to recognise the differences. For collective purpose, the typical time horizon would be whole life, whereas for mission ("How do we define our business?") it is ten years plus. In the case of vision ("What do we want for ourselves and for our key stakeholders?"), it is five years plus.

Collective purpose has taken centrestage as a critical issue for individuals and organisations in the world today. Its relevance to Asian leaders is, if anything, becoming more relevant than ever before. So for many organisations, a reexamination or reaffirmation of collective purpose seems right for the times; we have witnessed a global financial crisis brought about by a confluence of different factors, among which morality and the true role of business have been called into question by many around the world. Hence, it seems opportune for us to reflect on our respective common purposes.

Across Asia, in contrast to Europe and North America, the recession has had a relatively short-lived, mild or even largely unnoticed effect: growth rate projections continue to rise, the great Asian urban conurbations continue with their restless buzz and Asian corporations continue to extend their influence further into Africa and Latin America. In a sense, one could argue that a reappraisal of our existing capitalist or neo-capitalist mercantile system, especially the banking system — touted by many in Europe and North America as being urgent and necessary — could be judged as an overreaction or deemed irrelevant by many in Asia. Some would say that Asia has taken it all in its stride and moved on.

But that would be to miss an opportunity that Asian leaders now have before them: to reappraise and reevaluate the applicability in an Asian context of so-called Western models of business, especially when it comes to morality and ethics in business, and to offer up, with greater confidence than ever before, radical alternatives and perspectives that even non-Asian organisations might embrace to their benefit. They have an opportunity to challenge the status quo on management thinking. Common purpose is a good place to start this reappraisal.

One way to proceed is to use purpose to initiate mindset and strategic change. A revisiting of collective purpose or a reappraisal of how we inspire collective meaning making (why are we here, doing what we are doing?) provides us with the possibility of crafting strategies that are based on core values that deliver tangible results.

The purpose is the starting point for enabling strategic outcomes that are measurable and "real" in a way that appeal to results-driven Asian and non-Asian leaders in Asia and beyond. In other words, establishing or restating collective purpose is something that companies and organisations can and must do if they are to be the best.

In their book, *Built to Last*, Collins and Porras note that the founder of Johnson & Johnson, Robert W. Johnson, as far back as 1935, stated his philosophy of "enlightened self-interest" whereby:

> "service to *customers* [his italics] comes first ... service to *employees and management* comes second, and ... service to *stockholders* last."

In research conducted by Roffey Park in the UK, results showed that organisations that focused exclusively on shareholder value as a driver of purpose were not as successful as those which had a customer-oriented common or collective purpose. This suggests that those organisations that are able to identify the main drivers of their common purpose (whether customer orientation, employee engagement, reputation in the community or, indeed, shareholder or stakeholder value) and that can find a way to connect them all, if that works for them, will be in a great position to answer the question "Why are we here?" in a way that makes sense to its people.

The worst performers were those where shareholder value and collective purpose were co-mingled or confused — a bit of both but in all cases, lacking the clarity which a collective purpose demands. In our world today, we can see the results of an overemphasis on shareholder-driven strategy: less than ideal employee engagement, poor levels of trust and, in many cases, abhorrence by the consumer of whole sectors of the commercial world. The situation has significant implications for leadership from a moral stand-point and, worryingly, for critical business issues such as talent management and the talent pipeline. Those from Generation Y and younger are undoubtedly more ques-tioning of the values of the organisation for which they might consider working, so even for Asian companies enjoying boom times in an environment of consumer frenzy (where the appetite is for more and better goods and services), ignoring the longer-term impact and implication of a poorly articulated or worse, largely unnoticed, collective purpose will threaten the sustainability of the organisation itself. The message is clear: we need to pay attention now before it is too late. The CEO of Dr Reddy's in India said recently that he felt the company needed to revisit and refocus its core, collective purpose. So the change was made from "Helping people lead healthier lives" to "Providing affordable and innovative medicines for healthier lives".

Statements about collective purpose should stay in place because they are intended to withstand the passage of time (because they answer the question "Why are we here?"), but as times change, the case for a reappraisal of the collective purpose can be made with reasonable justification. A change in collective purpose will also entail a reappraisal or restatement of the values underpinning the purpose, and will trigger off either a subtle or potentially radical change in the organisation's overall strategic thrust.

Research carried out by Springett with Roffey Park (2004) posits the idea that a customer-focused purpose leads to both a strategic and creative capability inside an organisation, in contrast to a purpose which maximises only shareholder value. A purpose which maximises shareholder value will provide a strategic focus, but it will not enable "sufficient investment in people or creative capability" (Springett, 2004). It also means that the employees of organisations which concentrate solely on shareholder value as a purpose typically say that they would like to see more meaning in their work lives.

Implications For Asian Leaders

Why should Asian leaders reflect deeply and act on collective purpose? The answer is that strong collective purpose is related not only to organisational performance but importantly, to sustainable financial success ("the bottom line"). Research underscores the tight correlation between leadership that is judged excellent or exemplary with strong collective purpose.

At the same time, uniting employees in a common purpose is still an underdeveloped area for many organisations. Employees need to believe that the organisation they work for has a higher purpose, that they can do something worthwhile for others, especially their customers, and that their organisation has a role to play in society in a wider sense. A solid collective purpose must emphasise values; if it does, people respond to it. They feel that their work matters and has meaning.

So what can leaders do to ensure that collective purpose lives and thrives in their organisations? Three actions come to mind. The first and critical thing is to distinguish purpose from mission or vision, and then to make *communication of the purpose easy and frequent.* Employees need to be able to say why they do what they do. This is less about capturing the purpose neatly in a framed poster and hanging it on the wall, and more about modelling appropriate behaviours as a leader role model.

The second is that we ensure that *the brand mirrors the purpose.* When employees see their organisation's brand, they know and understand the purpose and can communicate it in their behaviours and deeds.

The third is to consider how to go about *measuring the impact of a strong collective purpose.* There are various ways to get at this. One is to conduct employee engagement surveys and track the trends over time. High employee engagement should translate into a healthy bottom line. Another is to conduct regular checks on how clients or customers view your organisation. These methods can help ensure that you stay on track.

Broad Lessons Learned

Having a strong sense of collective purpose brings tangible benefits to an organisation. We can expect to see higher levels of employee engagement and through this, a link to enhanced performance, that is, a happier, more engaged workforce which is more productive and, therefore, with potential for improved results (financial and non-financial). A strong sense of purpose can imbue teams with an almost spiritual feeling; so while they are working (in the majority of cases) for a positive (financial) outcome, there is more to work than simply revenue: they can feel that they are contributing to society in a broader sense. This is uplifting not only from a morale perspective but also, critically, from a *moral* perspective.

Strong collective purpose can also be thought of as "the ties that bind". Teams united behind a common or collective purpose enjoy cohesiveness and a sense of direction that elude those that are not "together". A report by the Chartered Institute for Personnel Development (CIPD) in the UK (2009) quotes Phil Jackson, former coach to Michael Jordan and the Chicago Bulls, as saying:

> "The most effective way to forge a winning team is to call on the players' need to connect with something larger than themselves. Even for those who do not consider themselves 'spiritual' in a conventional sense, creating a successful team — whether it's an NBA champion or a record-setting sales force — is essentially a spiritual act. It requires the individuals involved to surrender their self-interest for the greater good so that the whole adds up to more than the sum of its parts."

The same report by the CIPD also underscores the view that shared purpose drives organisational performance. Bevan (2005) and Buytendijk (2006) found that high-performing organisations have a strong sense of shared purpose internally and with their external stakeholders.

The broad lessons for leaders in Asia are, therefore, to review carefully their purpose. In some cases, the purpose will need to be changed, as it was by Dr Reddy's in India. Leaders will need to consider whether the purpose aptly reflects the aspirations of the company to be the kind of place where people wish to work and to direct their efforts: does the purpose provide meaning in the workplace? Leaders may also like to ask themselves the question: does our purpose reflect the moral authority of the senior leadership? Does trust exist?

One way to surface common purpose is to try asking deep questions, an approach suggested by Adrian Lock (2010) at Roffey Park. He has enumerated a number of questions that can help organisations focus on the right things to be thinking about when defining or redefining purpose. The questions are:

1. What is our unique "Voice" in the marketplace and the world?
2. What legacy do we want to leave in the lives of our clients?
3. What legacy do we want to leave in the lives of our employees?
4. What legacy do we want to leave in the world at large?
5. What drives us fundamentally?
6. What do we really, really want?

Finding the right answers to these questions will set up a chain reaction that will help leaders to be effective and successful. A solid, common purpose leads to organisational clarity (it answers the question: why are we here, doing what we are doing?); it gives people the sense that they are working for higher order ideals, not just for money, prestige or self-aggrandisement. From a solid purpose comes a solid strategy and from that, clarity around what the organisation needs to focus on in terms of goals and objectives (at a more tactical level).

While it is still too early to tell, the signs are that organisations that are able to articulate their purpose in a trustful and meaningful way will be the ones that ultimately attract the best talent from the younger generation starting to enter the workforce of the future.

References

Bevan, S., M. Cowling, H. Horner, N. Isles and N. Turner. (2005). *Cracking the Performance Code: How Firms Succeed*. London: The Work Foundation.

Buytendijk, F. (2006). The five keys to building a high-performance organisation. *Business Performance Management*, (February):24–30.

Chartered Institute of Personnel and Development (CIPD). (2009). *Shared Purpose and Sustainable Organisation Performance: Shaping the Future*. London: CIPD.

Collins, J. and Porras, J. (2005). *Built to Last: Successful Habits of Visionary Companies* (New edition). London: Random House.

Holbeche, L. and N. Springett. (2004). *In Search of Meaning in the Workplace*. Horsham, UK: Roffey Park Institute.

Lock, A. (2010). *The Organisational Deep Questions Model*. Horsham, UK: Roffey Park Institute (work in progress).

PART SIX

Capitalising on Capability

20

Purpose-inspired Leadership

Deb Henretta

Seven million times a month, every month, the word "Leadership" is typed into Google. If you add this to all the times that someone typed in a phrase that had "leadership" in it, like "Strategic Leadership" or "Effective Leadership", that number swells to more than 10 million.

That is a lot of people looking for leadership.

And to each of those queries, there is a bewildering array of answers. Google returns as many as 130 million entries on leadership!

Fortunately for me, I work for a company which has a simple, straightforward view of leadership. A view that is deeply rooted in our company's Purpose.

The Power of Purpose

Our Purpose calls on us to touch and improve the lives of the world's consumers, now and for generations to come. On the surface, Proctor & Gamble's (P&G) Purpose may sound similar to what other companies have — a mantra or a feel-good slogan. But at P&G, it is far more than that.

For me, it provides a daily, weekly and monthly guide to the work we do at P&G to deliver on business goals, such as sales growth, share growth and cash productivity. We know, and history has been witness, that when we keep our focus on touching and improving the lives of more consumers, in more parts of the world, more completely, we deliver on our business goals; we grow and we thrive.

So thanks to our Purpose, I come to work thinking about how I can help more mothers across Asia provide better care for their babies. I come to work thinking about how to improve the chances of survival for the children of Asia via P&G's Children's Safe Drinking Water programme and our Pampers vaccination programme. I think about improving the quality of their education by developing plans to expand our P&G-sponsored "Hope" Schools in China and our "Shiksha" Schools in India.

Being able to link my work as a leader to a greater purpose gives my organisation and me a sense of *personal* purpose. It *drives* us towards a greater common good. It creates a community of people who are committed to take the lead in making a difference. And when everybody is inspired to lead the way, leadership becomes an easy sail.

This is the power of purpose. And some of the world's greatest leaders bear testimony to this.

Lee Kwan Yew had a purpose. He wanted to see Singapore rise from a small island with a colonial past to a beacon of prosperity and 21st century success. His purpose inspired a generation of Singaporeans who worked to shape their country into the pride of Asia. Today, Minister Mentor Lee is recognised as one of the world's great leaders. I have had the good fortune of meeting him a few times and every time, I have come away with a drive to do more, to see more possibilities and to lead more positive change.

In my work on the Business Council for Asia-Pacific Economic Cooperation, I had the privilege of working with Jack Ma, one of the most recognised business leaders in China. Ma is a stellar example of a purpose-inspired leader. He is a visionary who saw the power of the Internet and the far-reaching impact it could have for China. He made it his purpose to empower Chinese men and women to connect, communicate and transact, to sync themselves, their lives and their businesses into a digital world that demands rapid adoption and engagement. Today, Ma's Alibaba, a business-to-business marketplace site, serves more than 40 million members from more than 240 countries and territories. His business is ever expanding and now includes five business entities, including Alibaba. com, Taobao.com, Alipay.com, Alibaba Cloud Computing and China Yahoo.

Purpose-inspired Culture

I really believe that human beings are wired to search for meaning in their lives and work. That's why a Purpose like P&G's can be so inspiring. The opportunity to touch and improve billions of people's lives every day is an inspiration that is exponentially more motivating than any inspiration that an individual leader may provide.

From an organisational standpoint, believing in the power of Purpose to lead people to action involves creating a culture of personal responsibility.

Every P&G employee has a role to play. Each one of them sees a personal opportunity and responsibility to make a difference. The senior management of the company and I try to ensure that there is a clear line of sight between our Purpose, our company strategies, our business and function strategies, and each individual's work plan. No one at P&G should be unclear about how and where to contribute. Everyone contributes in some way to P&G's consumer knowledge, innovation and brand-building capabilities, go-to-market capability and global scale. Everyone is responsible for disciplined execution and responsible stewardship of the Company's resources. And, ultimately, everyone plays a part in fulfilling P&G's Purpose which enables us to deliver the business and financial results shareholders deserve and that we expect of one another.

For example, P&G's Purpose to touch and improve lives means there are many opportunities to work on brands that meet basic needs like health and hygiene in developing countries. In India, being focused on improving lives makes a young Assistant Brand Manager work on projects that makes sanitary napkins accessible to rural women in India, reduces infection and improves their productivity. She leads specific projects every day that she sees connect back to our Purpose.

This culture of personal responsibility is directly linked to leadership: personal leadership.

The Culture of Personal Leadership

For me, the greatest achievement of a leader is not how many followers he or she has but rather, how many leaders he or she creates. It is what I call the legacy of leadership.

A powerful purpose has the ability to shape a culture where people are self-motivated leaders united in their desire to realise a common dream. A powerful purpose creates a culture of personal leadership and mobilises whole groups of people to exceed their individual definitions of success.

Successful leaders must begin with their people. Our former President and Chairman of P&G, Richard Dupree, once said:

> "If you leave us our money, our buildings and our brands but take away our people, the Company will fail. But if you take away our money, our buildings and our brands but leave us our people, we can rebuild the whole thing in a decade."

At P&G, we realised early on that people are our greatest asset. To tap the full potential of our employees, we developed a rigorous and disciplined approach to leadership development in every region and at every level of the company. Bob McDonald, P&G Chairman and CEO, explains why this is a strategic priority:

> "We hold ourselves accountable at P&G not only for attracting top talent, but also for providing the experiences, coaching, training and relationships that ensure people grow to their full potential as leaders. This pays enormous dividends because when people develop the skills to lead and are then inspired by our Purpose, they do great things."

The Impact of Purpose-inspired Leadership

The whole idea of nurturing a culture of leadership that begins and ends with our Purpose is so rewarding because it allows us to lead in ways that a more traditional notion of business leadership would not. We are, of course, proud that P&G is the global leader in the consumer products industry.

But we are equally proud that P&G takes decisions every day that makes it a leader in ways that improve life, like doing more in our social responsibility and environmental sustainability programmes.

We design more eco-friendly packaging, such as our compact liquid detergents that use less water, less packaging and require less shipping. Since 2002, we have delivered nearly 50% reduction in energy usage, CO_2 emissions and water usage in Asia alone. We have also been able to reduce our water and energy consumption by nearly 40% during this period. Many of these programmes also generate significant cost reductions that help drive profits.

Our social innovation projects, such as the Pampers vaccination programme, are helping to rid the world of neonatal tetanus. P&G's Children's Safe Drinking Water programme, powered by the innovation behind our PUR water-cleaning brand, is helping children in developing and underdeveloped countries of the world who do not have access to clean, safe drinking water get off to a healthy start.

PUR was inspired by our desire to save some of the 1.6 million children that die each year from dysentery. We knew that lives could be saved by providing clean, safe drinking water, but it required going beyond chlorine treatments that kill bacteria and viruses but do not kill deadly parasites. Through partnerships with the US Centers for Disease Control, we developed a technology that squeezed a multistep process used by water treatment plants into a small sachet of powder.

Today, with partners such as UNICEF and the World Health Organization, PUR has helped provide more than two billion litres of safe drinking water across more than

54 countries in the world. Last year, in Asia alone, PUR packets provided over 25 million litres of clean drinking water to disaster-struck communities in the Philippines and Indonesia.

All of these programmes are led by people who are inspired by our Purpose of touching and improving lives. And, in my mind, every single individual who is driven by a sense of personal commitment to realise a greater purpose has the potential to become a great leader.

21

Corporate Culture

Howard Thomas

T he culture of an organisation can be described as:

> "the underlying assumptions, beliefs and values in an organisation which inform, influence and shape strategic decision making."

The influence of organisation culture on decision making reveals what is often taken for granted in decision making processes. The impact of organisation culture often goes unnoticed by members of an organisation. Culture is continually reinforced by symbols, stories and routines, as well as by organisational structures and the power plays of various interests. Culture tends to be self-reinforcing. In addition, culture provides a set of values which are reflected in choice behaviours and processes. Schein (1992) shows how decision making is influenced both by artefacts and basic assumptions held by individuals in organisations, as illustrated in Figure 21.1.

Figure 21.1 Artefacts and assumptions in strategic decision making

Assumption	Value-led decision making	Artefact
Example: Taken for granted beliefs	Example: Goals and strategies	Example: Organisation structures
Perceptual habits (ways of thinking)	Answers to the question "why?"	Technologies
Basic attitudes	Vision and mission	Jargon and dress code

Source: Adapted from Schein (1992).

Organisational culture, therefore, colours decision making from a palette that can include such things as ritual and language, alongside the influence of technology and organisational structure. These factors all intermingle to colour decisions that we would be tempted to otherwise view as rational choices. The cultural perspective shows how values are added to the decision process. Sometimes, such values are overt. They can be seen in mission statements such as Yamaha's "Kill Honda", Federal Express's "Absolutely on Time", Far East Organization's "Inspiring Better Lives" or 3M's "To Solve Unsolved Problems Innovatively". At other times, values can be shaped by taken for granted behaviours, jargon or dress codes (for example, we all wear business suits in sober colours exemplified by financial markets across the world: New York, London, Singapore and Hong Kong). These are more covert influences.

Simpler versions of how strategic decisions are influenced by the context or culture of organisations can be found in the work of Jim Collins and Jerry Porras (1996). They argued that successful companies were those where the core decisions were influenced by timeless guiding principles which require no external justification. This cherished core ideology represents the key values of the organisation and is the cultural glue that holds it together in the face of other changes. So long as key decisions were taken in line with these cherished principles, outstanding performance over a sustained period was the result. In essence, strong core ideology and culture can be a core capability for long-term competitive advantage.

However, organisations can also become trapped by their coherent cultures into routines which impair the development of new and different strategies, impede strategic change and lessen the ability to sustain a distinctive, competitive advantage. The practice of strategic decision making, therefore, becomes constrained rather than enhanced by the organisational culture. Decision makers can only think along the rigid lines demarcated by the strong culture. Innovation and creative thinking are precluded and invoking learning into the organisation becomes very difficult, since the culture resists new ideas.

Decision makers, therefore, have to be very clear whether the culture of the organisation is working for its success, or is actually constraining choice activities. Spotting the difference can be very difficult since the choice-enhancing factors identified by Collins and Porras very closely resemble the "mindguards" that can detract from innovative thinking. The advantage of corporate culture is that it provides a set of key assumptions and values that guide strategic decision making. However, the culture may have to be adapted in strategic change through organisational learning.

Culture and Learning

Writers such as Peter Senge (1998) stress and emphasise the role of processes of learning and adaptability in organisations with regard to understanding the pace of strategic change, and in providing new ways of conceptualising the business environment. Thus, strategists can frame strategic issues in terms of the web of customers and stakeholders in order to manage the business better (create more value).

Senge emphasises the importance of what he calls "adaptive learning" and "generative learning" in organisations. Adaptive learning is similar to what Argyris and Schon (1978) call "single-loop" learning in which individuals, groups and organisations adjust their behaviour according to fixed organisational goals, norms and assumptions. Generative learning, on the other hand, is akin to "double-loop" learning, in which organisational goals, norms and assumptions as well as behaviour are all open to change, particularly in contexts characterised by threats of technological or regulatory change. Developing "double-loop" learning is critical for cultural adaptation and effective strategy execution. In Senge's terms:

> "Increasing adaptiveness is only the first stage in moving towards learning organisations. The impulse to learn in children goes deeper than desires to respond and adapt more effectively to environmental change. The impulse to learn, at its heart, is an impulse to be generative, to expand our capability. This is why leading corporations are focusing on generative learning, which is about creating, as well as adaptive learning, which is about coping."

Therefore, Senge is wedded to the idea of the firm both as a system and a social and knowledge web, which is conceptually very close to Arie de Geus's (1988) framing of the firm as the "living company". This "living company" survives over the long term through such concrete factors as financial strength and stability, environmental sensitivity and adaptation to change, as well as a strong culture, identity and value system which enable it to become a systematic, living organism that continually grows and reinvents itself. Leaders of such organisations are "systems thinkers" who see the "big picture" and focus more on understanding the underlying reasons and forces that contribute to change. Important skills for such leaders, exemplified by the example of Nissan in Chapter 11, include:

1. The ability to see the interrelationships and processes in systemic change.
2. The recognition that problems in change result from poorly designed systems.
3. The ability to recognise and understand the dynamic complexity of system problems, that is, when the cause and effect of strategic problems are distant in time and space, and when the consequences of interventions over time are subtle.
4. The ability to focus on areas of high leverage, that is, systems thinking shows that small, well-focused actions can produce significant, enduring improvements if they are in the right place.
5. The avoidance of symptomatic solutions, that is, "quick fixes" or so-called "band-aid solutions". The best solutions rely on the ability to analyse the system and, thus, find enduring solutions. Enduring solutions create value.

Far East Organization, led by Philip Ng, is a strong example of leadership which sees the "big picture". Over the last 50 years, it has transformed from an entrepreneur-led organisation (a family business) to a strong, local Singapore company and has more recently spread its reach to alliances in Hong Kong and the acquisition of a food and beverage company, Yeo Hiap Seng Ltd. In this growth, it has emphasised an entrepreneurial culture, team organisation and service excellence. It is an example of how, through leadership, a local company has adapted and kept multinationals at bay. In particular, the Far East Organization has a business model which has adapted to local needs and scope, and thus gained competitive advantage. Further, it has invested in talent and encouraged an entrepreneurial spirit and good customer stewardship.

Culture and Value: Trust and Reputation

The following issues are core cultural and critical intangible assets for the implementation and execution of strategy: trust and reputation/image/identity.

Trust

This involves creating a strong sense of mission and values. Collins and Porras (1996) note that core values are enduring, essential tenets for those inside the organisation. The core ideology consists of core values and core purpose, where core purpose is the *raison d'etre* — the reason for being. Core ideology has to be authentic and is the "glue" that holds the organisation together over time. It is a consistent identity that all stakeholders learn to trust over time. For example, Hewlett-Packard's (HP) core ideology was a code of ethics called the "HP Way". It includes:

1. A deep respect for the individual.
2. A dedication to affordable quality and reliability.
3. A commitment to community responsibility.
4. HP exists to make technical contributions for the advancement and welfare of humanity.

Note that trust needs to be earned, but can be easily lost. Johnson and Johnson's (J&J) use of its credo, its core ideology, to handle the recall of its Tylenol pain relievers in 1982 is a well-cited example of a reinforcement of trust with consumers and a victory for crisis management. J&J's action was simple, right and it worked. But it happened a generation ago!

Contrast this with the sorry response of Toyota to very recent complaints about safety and faulty designs with its Lexus and Toyota cars, particularly in the USA. Toyota has somewhat lost the trust of consumers because its relentless growth reinforced its rather conservative culture. Its overconfidence in its own technology, corporate size, bureaucratic culture and lack of openness to divergent views made it inertial and insensitive to changes taking place both in its internal and external environments. The response of Akio Toyoda, President of Toyota, has been much criticised and for him, sorry was the hardest word to say.

Reputation, Imagination and Identity

"Reputation, reputation, reputation — the one immortal part of man." (Shakespeare, from *Othello*)

The modern, resource-based theory of the firm identifies a range of intangible assets including technology, patents and skills which, when combined with human and organisational resources, define the firm's core dynamic capabilities or core competencies in the process of strategic execution. A key set of intangible assets are the firm's reputational assets and these include the company name, its identity, brands, brand image and customer-based loyalty, the reputation of the firm's products and services, and the integrity of its relationships with the complex web of customers, suppliers, communities and governments.

Many of the world's top brands (such as Coca-Cola, Microsoft, Toyota, IBM, GE, Singapore Airlines, Intel and Nescafe) are household names and help to develop a strong relationship of value, trust and goodwill with the customer. As we have recently seen, however, in the accounting industry, with the demise of Arthur Andersen, a hard-won reputation was easily dissipated and lost by the unethical and illegal behaviour of its employees. And, in the case of Toyota's recent safety problems, reputational damage to its brand and identity has taken place. Therefore, a strong corporate reputation is a key strategic asset in managing corporate culture and achieving distinctiveness in competition.

Lessons Learned about Corporate Culture and Core Ideology from Corporate Leaders

The strongest cultural aspect mentioned was the relevance of certain Asian cultural characteristics as impediments to strategic change and effective strategic execution. It was recognised that Asian managers have strong cultural values: for example, an outstanding work ethic, excellent mathematical, analytic talent and capability, and a deep sense of humility. However, they exhibit a number of cultural, capability gaps. These include a strong acceptance of hierarchy and authority ("What the Boss says goes!"), an aversion to risk-taking and making mistakes, a lack of engagement in constructive dialogue and debate in decision making groups, and an inadequate global mindset and understanding of diversity in international arenas.

They stressed the need for a much more empowered culture and a sense that a set of evolving and changed cultural values were necessary to reflect openness to change and more engaged employees. This was necessary in order to leverage the basic, outstanding and strategic human capital, and to train them to develop the leadership characteristics and capabilities to compete effectively in the Asian marketplace. This would include the design of leadership teams and sharing of important managerial practices across those teams.

Key questions that arise in capitalising on culture to improve organisational core competencies are:

1. How should an organisation generate understanding of the core values and ideologies in its culture?
2. Can culture be a source of sustainable, competitive advantage?
3. How should managers work effectively in the context of an organisation's culture?
4. Can corporate culture be transformed and modified? Can barriers to the effective management of diversity be removed in order to achieve a global mindset?
5. How can new managerial talent be successfully absorbed into an organisation's culture?

References

Argyris, C. and D.A. Schon. (1978). *Organisation Learning: A Theory of Action Perspective*. Reading, MA: Addison-Wesley.

Bhattacharya, A.K. and D.C. Michael. (2008). How local companies keep multi-nationals at bay. *Harvard Business Review*, (March):84–95.

Collins, J. and Porras, J. (1996). *Built to Last*. New York: Century Books.

de Geus, A. (1988). Planning as learning. *Harvard Business Review*, (March/April):70–5.

Schein, E.H. (1992). *Organizational Culture and Leadership* (2nd edition). San Francisco: Jossey-Bass.

Senge, P. (1998). The leader's new work: building learning organisations. In: S. Segal-Horn (Ed.), *The Strategy Reader* (pp. 296–312). Oxford: Blackwell.

When sorry is the hardest word. *Financial Times*, 29 April 2010.

Multiculture versus Company Culture

Michael Jenkins

The Principles

The issue of multiculturalism is challenging and endemic. Businesses are becoming globalised, cross-border migration is increasing and technology is reducing trade barriers. Organisations large and small, international and national are employing people from different cultures and selling to customers across the world. We are living in an increasingly complex world. In order to gain maximum brand engagement, companies need to understand and embrace different cultural norms, appealing to markets on a global scale and enabling employees, who have different backgrounds and beliefs, to perform well together. This raises a number of issues for organisations: how to understand a complex market; the cross-cultural issues that could impact strategy; employees' response to mergers and acquisitions; managing across borders, time zones and cultures; and achieving high performance from a diverse workforce.

Corporate Culture versus National Culture

Corporate culture is often described in the organisational setting as "the way we do things around here", and it can be a very strong influence in some companies. For example, in Toyota, all employees receive induction in the Toyota Way. It enables an organisation to have consistency of message and brand, and can be a reason people choose to join the company. Schein (1992) describes corporate culture as having three levels:

1. *Surface level.* The visible manifestations, such as corporate branding, symbols, behaviours and structures.
2. *Mid level.* This is driven by values and beliefs.
3. *Deep level.* This is driven by some basic assumptions about how the organisation works.

Managers (and individual employees) bring their personal cultural norms from their family upbringing, their education, their previous work experience and their nationality to their role in leading others. Laurent (1986) found that nationality had three times more influence on shaping managerial assumptions than any other characteristic.

National culture has been the subject of much research, with Hofstede (2003), Gesteland (2005) and Trompenaars and Hampden-Turner (1997) suggesting different dimensions that can be used for cultural analysis. Critics of this approach have argued that in today's globalised world with increased cross-cultural exposure, the cultural dimensions proposed are less relevant. Nevertheless, it would be unwise to ignore ethnicity and suggest that everyone can be managed in exactly the same way.

Whilst a collective purpose might provide a common goal, different people expect different rewards and recognition. Acknowledging individual differences in ability and personality traits may be important in a North American meritocracy, whilst recognition of team results might be pertinent in a Japanese manufacturing firm. Openness to understanding different ethnic (national and religious) cultures is a useful starting point for leaders seeking to build organisational consistency, whilst also appreciating the value of cultural differences.

Implications For Asian Leaders

How Do Leaders Find a Way Through the National versus Corporate Culture Debate?

Leaders in Asia need to take a broad view of diversity and a multicultural lens is useful when considering business strategy and the related HR strategy. If an organisation is to attract diverse talent with the innovative thinking and creativity to create a unique proposition, it will need to appeal to a wide audience. The goal for a leader in Asia is to attract people who are culturally sensitive both to national and corporate cultures. This may mean attracting people who can work effectively locally, but who also feel comfortable in a highly matrixed, international environment too.

How Does a Leader Become More Multicultural or Culturally Aware?

Being multicultural or being culturally aware is a mixture of nature and nurture. People who have grown up in a multilingual family, or a country where diversity is marked, are often better placed to develop themselves as culturally sensitive leaders in their professional lives. That said, growing up in a monocultural environment does not preclude people from learning about other cultures and other ways of thinking. The known element is that leaders and managers in Asia need to be credible leaders who can engage and motivate their followers, whatever the culture their followers come from. This is something that requires exceptional skill and probably grows from experience derived from extensive travel, an experimental mindset and an adaptive and flexible approach to learning.

Research into managing teams across cultures (Sinclair and Robertson-Smith, 2008) highlights the challenges. Multicultural teams have greater potential for misunderstandings and conflict, which are exacerbated if team members are dispersed geographically and across time zones. A leader in Asia needs to factor this into his or her strategic planning and approach to people development.

How Should a Leader Behave? How Do Leaders Need to Think and Act?

Leaders need to be good communicators, using a variety of media to get their message across. They need to be adept at encouraging participation and managing performance. They also need to be open-minded and able to suspend their assumptions about the way things have been done historically; they need to be prepared to set aside managerial methods that have been tried and tested in the past, and to try other ideas and approaches. Leaders need high levels of emotional intelligence to be both self-aware and have the interpersonal sensitivity to develop relationships based on trust and credibility. This takes time and patience.

How Do Leaders Need to Work With Multicultural Teams?

Developing an effective multicultural team requires investment at the beginning of a project to build working relationships. Time spent face to face is essential in establishing expectations; there may be varying attitudes to time management and the perceived purpose of meetings. Decision making protocols will need to be discussed to avoid any confusion and norms established about expected levels of participation in debates. Different cultures have different expectations about formality or informality, and inappropriate humour can cause offence. People need to understand how to express divergent views without losing friendship or respect. A management style of guidance rather than direction appears to work well, as it allows for exploration of knowledge and expertise and demonstrates respect for the experience people bring to the team.

Members of multicultural teams need to learn to work together, so they can communicate effectively, recognise levels of language ability, and openly discuss different ways of working. The manager needs to use different motivational techniques to achieve results, and understand how to deal with poor performance without causing loss of face. Facilitation skills will enable a manager to deal with conflict and help team members to reach an understanding of the problem. The leader has to decide when to develop consensus, and when to lead from the front, when to keep their distance and when to offer hands-on support. This challenge is amplified when the team is dispersed across a region and face-to-face meetings are infrequent. Regular reporting has to be set up in such a way that it does not imply a lack of trust and the manager needs the ability to offer both support and coaching from a distance.

A leader has to be open-minded and ready to explore cultural difference, recognising that it can help to achieve greater durability and innovation. The leader has a key role to play if the team is to achieve superior performance; they need to appreciate the complexity of their role and remain flexible and open to adjusting their behaviour to meet the needs of the team, being a guide and a facilitator rather than an authoritarian figurehead — and at all times, providing a sense of direction and purpose.

Broad Lessons Learned

Organisations in Asia that have successfully met the challenges of and built on the opportunities presented by multiculturalism typically make use of a variety of different approaches, tactics and practices.

One of the principal areas requiring attention is that of raising cultural awareness and understanding inside the organisation and at the team level. There are various excellent providers of cross-cultural awareness training that help participants to work through issues, such as how to go about understanding another culture, how to appreciate other ways of thinking, how to appreciate the ways in which their own culture might differ from those of other team members, and how to overcome or work around language and cultural barriers.

Most specialists in the field of cross-cultural awareness training would agree that knowledge of how different cultures interact has increased significantly over the last decade. The training is more likely to look at the deeper meanings of culture and less likely to dwell on the more manifestly different aspects, such as body language and hand gestures, although these still have a place in some instances.

Participants of cross-cultural awareness training are more likely to see these programmes related to or integrated with broad-based leadership or management programmes. The questions are now more likely to be around how a coach interacts with a coachee when neither shares the same language or culture, or about thinking through how decision making might happen in a collective, multicultural team environment.

Sometimes, companies organise a development experience where the focus is on understanding leadership dynamics rather than multicultural dynamics: the participating group is multicultural and the lessons are learned through in-the-moment interaction with each other while participating in activities designed to highlight a particular leadership competence or practice. Having a facilitator who is both a leadership expert and a cross-cultural specialist can be enormously helpful in helping a group or team to think through and reflect on what they learned, and how they intend to use the experience back in the workplace. One way to further support this kind of learning is to alternate training venues across the respective team members' countries, if time and money allow.

A second principal area for attention is that of conflict management. Misunderstandings about different points of view, values and priorities will undoubtedly impact the effectiveness of multicultural teamwork. Conflict, and wondering about how to deal with it, is frequently the reason why a multicultural team resorts to cross-cultural training! It is often helpful for the manager of a team to clarify the roles of each member of the team from the outset in order to mitigate the potential for conflict around role and responsibility later on. This is most usefully done in a one-to-one way because it allows each member of the multicultural team to ask questions in his or her own time.

Some successful Chinese multinationals have found that rigorously observed "rules of engagement" for multicultural team meetings can mean the difference between harmony and success, friction and disaster. For example, being clear about whether the meeting is intended to convey information, to ask for ideas or to seek consensus can be very useful in framing the interaction and makes it a more efficient and effective way of working. Allowing colleagues whose first language is different from yours (when yours is the language of the meeting) to develop their thesis or position early in the meeting (without interruption) can be very helpful to ensure that the meeting has a positive outcome.

These are all relatively small and sensible things to do, but it is surprising how they are often forgotten in the high speed, fast moving business environment in Asian countries. Experience shows that taking time to get these ground rules firmly established is a good way to work in a multicultural environment.

A third area for consideration is mutual respect. Encouraging people to be respectful of the opinions of others, and being courteous when sharing one's own views and perspectives, is a great way to build harmony in the team. The leader of the multicultural team needs to constantly monitor the preferred levels of participation of the group (and not assume that silence is either tacit consent or that the person simply does not have an opinion!). It is also helpful to let the members of the team know that, in the event of a breakdown in the group's ability for group members to communicate effectively amongst themselves, the help of a third party will be invoked in order to facilitate understanding and a return to cordial relations.

Finally, Asian managers will encounter situations where there is a fine line between balancing their own principles with what seems to be appropriate in a different culture and location. That is why it is important that the company or organisation provides employees with clear guidelines around company procedures and the ethics expected of them. These will not always provide the "answers" to every situation, but they go a long way to ensuring that good governance is practised.

References

Gesteland, R.R. (2005). *Cross-cultural Business Behaviour: Negotiating, Selling, Sourcing and Managing Across Cultures* (4th edition). Denmark: Copenhagen Business School Press.

Hofstede, G. (2003). *Cultures and Organizations: Software of the Mind* (3rd edition). London: Profile Books.

Laurent, A. (1986). The cross-cultural puzzle of international human resource management. *Human Resource Management*, 25:91–102.

Schein, E.H. (1992). *Organizational Culture and Leadership* (2nd edition). San Francisco, CA: Jossey-Bass.

Sinclair, A. and G. Robertson-Smith. (2008). *Managing Teams Across Cultures*. Horsham, UK: Roffey Park Institute.

Trompenaars, F. and K. Hampden-Turner. (1997). *Riding the Waves of Culture: Understanding Cultural Diversity in Business* (2nd edition). London: Nicholas Brealey.

PART SEVEN

Developing Careers

23

Developing World-class Leaders at General Electric

Stuart L Dean

With the rise of the Asian economy, General Electric (GE) today has about 18% of its 300,000-strong workforce working in Asia. This number is set to grow. Being a global company, how does GE manage its multicultural workforce globally, transcend national cultures, adapt to a fast changing environment and stay at the top as the leader in the industries they compete in and in the area of leadership development?

Developing World-class Leaders

As professional employees growing in GE, we are measured on performance and values with equal importance. As we grow into more senior leadership, the requirements for leadership skills and expertise become more prominent, with continuous focus on performance and values.

At the heart of GE's leadership development is the GE Growth Values, which exemplify the behavioural standards expected of a GE leader. Leadership development at GE, to a large extent, is about driving behavioural change. The GE Growth Values provide talents across the globe a common mental map of what and how a successful and effective leader in GE would say and do in their work and in dealing with people, regardless of their background.

The GE Growth Values have evolved over time in tandem with changing business needs. Today, we have six Growth Values, which are essentially the standards of successful leadership behaviours at GE:

1. External focus
2. Clear thinker
3. Imagination and courage
4. Inclusiveness
5. Expertise
6. Global

GE believes that what gets measured gets done. Employees are measured on their job performance as well as the demonstration of the Growth Values.

GE develops training programmes to train its leaders in the skill sets of a Growth Leader. For instance, to help managers understand how to be an Inclusive Leader, every manager with direct reports is required to attend the one-day Inclusive Leader Workshop, a programme designed by GE Crotonville and then rolled out to the different regions in the world.

In Asia, faculties were certified to deliver the workshop to its Asian audience. At the sessions, participants learn various methods/approaches on how to engage employees and brainstorm on what they can do to connect and empower their respective teams, taking into consideration the local context. Asian role model leaders are invited to share their experience on how they apply the Growth Values in their leadership walk, with the participants in GE's cornerstone leadership classes held in Asia.

Career Management: Systems and Processes

With our diverse cultures and complexities of businesses, we manage careers at GE with a global approach coupled with regional execution to adapt to each unique business requirement. To implement this approach, we have various systems and processes that shape GE career management: Session C, performance management, leadership development and talent acceleration.

Session C and EMS

Session C is an internal formal process that takes place annually to ensure optimal organisation alignment. It is a multilevel organisation review process that covers:

1. Organisational performance
2. Coming year's organisational challenges and actions
3. Leadership assessment and individual performance, strengths and development needs
4. Early identification of high potential talent pool and appropriate development plans
5. Succession planning for key leadership positions
6. Key leadership training nominations
7. Corporate initiatives

GE businesses also customise their agenda to meet their specific business needs. It will roll up from the country level to the Chairman level.

The whole process starts with the employees filling out a document and submitting what we call "EMS", which is a standardised appraisal form completed by all employees, annually online. This document captures employees' accomplishments against goals set at the start of the year, strengths, development needs and career interests. It is also a focal point for career discussions. On top of that, it incorporates an internal resume to reflect the career history of each individual.

With this document from every employee, there is a company-wide digitised process to facilitate the discussion among the leaders. After submitting the EMS, the business leader and HR will come together to discuss about these individual EMS. Even though this is an annual activity, managers are encouraged to do a mid-year review with employees to make sure that employees are aware of their own strengths and development needs, and how they are tracking against their goals, in advance so that they have a chance to work on their goals and development needs before the final review. After the one-to-one discussion has occurred, the manager will release the EMS to the employee and start the face-to-face discussion on the results.

The business leader and the HR will then do an assessment of all the employees as an organisation, compare with their business goals and come up with a set of gaps and actions to be taken in the coming year. They have to put a presentation together to review with their own manager and HR. Our digitised system allows us to pull various reports and summary charts to help us do our Session C presentation.

This process helps GE employees have a voice in how their career is managed because it provides:

1. Candid feedback about job performance and values
2. Get coaching and direction from the manager
3. Discuss goals and expectations for the future
4. Verify that the employee and the manager agree on the contents of the EMS and the expectations for the following year.

Performance Management

In GE, we have a strong performance management culture. With integrity as the foundation, values must accompany demonstrated performance excellence in order to advance. Both values and performance are equally important.

Performance is measured against the goals and objectives agreed upon by both employee and manager at the start of the year. As such, each employee is measured according to his or her own merits.

Our set of GE Growth Values — namely, External Focus, Clear Thinker, Global Imagination and Courage, Inclusiveness and Expertise — is applicable globally. The uniqueness of this is that each value can be interpreted on a local context. We will measure based on the effectiveness of how the employee does on the local culture and approach.

The GE performance management process helps employees manage their careers by knowing how they are doing, and by having candid conversations with their business leaders when they need to improve.

Leadership Development

One of our key employee value propositions is leadership development. We look at both the corporate leadership programmes and what GE Global Learning offers, namely, Crotonville Executive Leadership, Cornerstone Leadership,

Essential Leadership Skills courses and business knowledge courses.

Common Leadership Development Programmes Across the World

To build a common leadership mindset and language across the globe as well as a strong learning culture, a common suite of leadership development programmes are developed and offered by the GE Global Learning centre at GE Crotonville based in New York to all different regions in the world.

As GE becomes more global, it has developed several regional learning centres in different regions around the world, with GE Crotonville as the epicentre of learning. In Asia, there are Crotonville Leadership Program Managers based in India (who is also the Crotonville Leader for the Asia-Pacific region), China, ASEAN, Japan, Korea and Australia to manage the delivery of the programmes in their respective countries/regions.

Crotonville Leadership programmes are designed by a global team with representatives from the different regions involved. Local faculties go through a certification process and are responsible for delivering the programmes in their local environment, taking into account the cultural and other local context.

The GE Growth Values have been instrumental in developing the core leadership traits amongst its leaders and, at the same time, allow flexibility for leaders from different regions to adapt to the local culture and context as long as the core values are maintained. The core contents of the leadership development programmes, rolled out with adaptation to the local context, help to build leaders who are aligned to the GE culture and expectations, regardless of where they come from.

For leadership programmes, there are programmes for fresh graduates and mid-career or experienced employees. Generally, leadership programmes combine meaningful job assignments with formal classroom studies over a course of two years. In Asia, our rotations may cut across GE businesses, providing trainees great experience in a relatively short duration. The common programmes in Asia are our Financial Management Program, Operations Management Leadership Program, Information Management Leadership Program and Commercial Leadership Program.

There are Corporate Audit Staff, Experienced Commercial Leadership Program, Human Resources Leadership Program and Experienced Financial Leadership Program for our experienced employees or new hires. The criteria for selection of the trainees in Asia may vary a little from our headquarters in the US. In Asia, we tend to select slightly more experienced trainees as it is proven that this profile is more successful in the programme.

How about employees who have not gone through any leadership programmes? We encourage employees to grow through lateral or vertical transfers within or across GE businesses. This will help them to grow their skills and competencies. They can decide to grow their career in depth and expertise, or choose to grow in breadth.

We have an internal job posting system to support this. It is called the Career Opportunity System (COS). All jobs have to be posted in COS so that employees will know what is out there. Employees will have to clear with their managers before they apply for the role.

In Asia, each business tends to be smaller compared to our headquarters in the US. Thus, there are many examples of employees moving across businesses for developmental or promotional assignments. This is especially so for the functions with transferable skills, such as finance, human resources, information technology and legal.

Of course, everyone will have equal opportunity to the Global Learning training courses depending on their training needs. As mentioned earlier, key leadership training nominations are done through Session C. For the other needs, they are identified and discussed through the Session C and the EMS process.

Cross-business Talent Acceleration Programme

On top of the great global processes that are helping to manage GE employees' careers, our international businesses still face a challenge because we do not grow our local talents fast enough to take on bigger roles located in regions outside the US. Collectively, we developed our talent acceleration programme in GE International. The programme has a standard structure, but allows us to incorporate modules to address our common local leadership gaps which may differ from region to region.

In this programme, we identify common development needs through executive assessments done for talented individuals. These assessments are done by trained independent Human Resources Leaders to provide objective assessments of the talents. Most often, the assessors become the coach for the talent and guide their assessees in creating development action plans, and remain engaged and follow up on the assessees' progress.

From the results, we define our content on learning and coaching. We also match suitable mentors for the talents so that they can learn from someone who may complement their development needs.

We also take this chance to expose the talents to various great leaders in the company, as well as allow opportunities for them to share and network.

Conclusion

In GE, we create a common language and platform where people know what is expected of them, and help them to bring people together to forge a common future ahead, regardless of the country, region and culture they come from.

What we do at GE is to help people find common grounds for them to collaborate with each other, and to help one another to succeed. We respect the cultural differences and the different backgrounds that people have, but leverage on the diversity and differences to help our people and business grow.

24

Career Development in IBM: A Whole-of-Company Approach

Cordelia Chung

"I believe the real difference between success and failure in a corporation can be very often traced to the question of how well the organization brings out the great energies and talents of its people." (Watson, Jr., 1963)

What Drives Career Management at IBM?

Career development at IBM is driven by the needs of a large, global company involved in a broad range of business activities at the cutting edge of the knowledge-based economy. Our framework for defining, developing and deploying talent at all levels in the company has been shaped by our core values and business, and is designed to address several key characteristics of IBM's operations: our organisational scale, the need to adapt and innovate in a changing business environment, and the aspirations and deep potential of our employees.

Driven by Scale

IBM employs close to 400,000 people worldwide across a wide range of cultures and businesses in 170 countries. In order for an organisation of such scope and global reach to operate and deliver reliably high standards to our clients everywhere, we need to have a good grasp of the core skills, roles, competencies, methodologies and values which are essential to our business, and these have to be comprehensively defined, regularly updated and consistently applied across our entire company, no matter where our people are in the world.

Management must have a holistic overview of the company's entire pool of talent and capabilities at any given time; this allows us to quickly identify and mobilise relevant skills and capabilities across our operating landscape, making sure the right teams are in the right places at the right time. This standardised, comprehensive, data-based approach to capability management helps us to make the most of business opportunities in a diverse, global environment.

Driven by Change

A decade ago, we saw change coming. The IT industry and broader economy were being transformed by the rising tide of global integration, by a new computing model and by new client needs for integration and innovation. In response, IBM changed the mix of our businesses towards higher-value, more profitable segments of the industry. IBM divested commoditising businesses, such as personal computers and hard disk drives, and strengthened our position through strategic investments and acquisitions in areas such as analytics, next-generation data centres, cloud computing and green solutions. IBM became a globally integrated enterprise, leveraging our scale to capture new growth. We shifted our resources towards building client relationships and employee skills, while positioning IBM for new market opportunities in emerging markets.

These technological and business trends resulted in a rise in demand for services based on rapidly deployable, complex combinations of different skill sets, as well as entirely new job roles that have not existed before. Client businesses now prefer versatile service teams that can go beyond technical excellence alone — with broad capabilities in multiple domains that can provide total, innovative solutions for their business activities — what Harvard researcher Ranjay Gulai has called "boundary-spanning skills".

Our expansion in the emerging markets, such as Asia, has also called upon different types of job roles and skill sets with varying needs in different territories. A rapidly evolving business environment means that IBM must count on solid processes to identify the relevant skills, develop new expertise and deploy competent personnel in a way that is flexible enough to respond effectively to a complex and dynamic future, where the lead time for businesses has become much shorter.

Driven by Aspiration

A large company such as IBM must also offer employees the best means to excel in their performance, whatever new challenges they may face anywhere, anytime. This is also the best way for our people to advance their careers in ways that benefit both the individual and the company as they progress.

It has been said of the business world that we have moved past the era of the Generalist (in the 1980s) and the Specialist (in the 1990s), and ours is now the era of the Versatilist, where the ability to intelligently apply one's arsenal of competencies and experience to a broad range of activities — including new and unexpected situations — is now a key competitive advantage. The lifespan for specific skills has become shorter; even in the technology industry, technical aptitude is no longer always sufficient. Of course, there will always be a role for deep specialists and leading experts in a given field, but few professions will remain permanent vocations for life. Indeed, most employees today do not expect to stay in the same job for life.

A new generation of employees, hailing from very different cultural backgrounds and with different career aspirations, have brought new expectations to the table. For instance, Generation Y employees have been observed to be motivated by more than just pay; they lean towards companies who nurture collaboration, personal growth and favour more open and flexible working cultures with a healthy work-life balance. The modern employee wants to be engaged, challenged and wants to excel at meaningful work that contributes to personal as well as business goals.

For some time, the trend in the business world has been to empower individuals to take more control over their own careers and plan their own growth trajectories, as well as for employees to broaden their portfolios, work experience and skill sets as they advance in their careers.

The IBM Approach

Expertise Taxonomy System

These powerful and interrelated driving forces have resulted in the need for a formal and comprehensive framework for managing expertise and developing careers at IBM. Around 1992, IBM began developing a "skills dictionary" to codify the skills that employees require. It has since evolved into what is today IBM's Expertise Taxonomy System (ETS), a company-wide database available on a website. It establishes a common language for all the different job roles, associated skills and competencies used across all business units in the company. This system guides the identification of the following elements:

1. *Competencies.* The system starts with competencies that are needed by all employees regardless of their job role, country or status. Also listed are competencies or behaviours demonstrated by top performers which are key indicators of success for high-performing employees, and which differentiate IBMers from competitor companies.

2. *Skills.* Skills are fundamental to specific job roles and enable employees to perform their daily tasks.

3. *Capabilities.* As employees grow their competencies, become enabled, build skills and gain new experiences, they develop multiple capabilities that clients value.

With the ETS, all IBMers are placed on a standardised and holistic framework; they can be benchmarked in terms of their skill sets, job roles and capabilities in relation to the rest of the company, regardless of geography or business division. Not only is this resource-efficient across a large and diverse multinational company, it also ensures consistency, facilitates communication and enables management across a vast global operation. Management has access to an immediate overview of the total pool of relevant capabilities within IBM at any one time, how these capabilities are distributed and where potential gaps may lie. We are then better able to guide deployment and developmental needs at the global, business and individual levels. This means being able to place the right person with the right skills at the right time, location and cost.

The ETS framework informs all aspects of IBM's career management, from recruitment and training to performance assessment and evaluation, career guidance, planning, leadership development and succession planning. There are 300,000 learning activities associated with the curriculum for competencies alone. A wide spectrum of skills-specific formal and on-the-job training programmes, job rotations, mentorships and stretch assignments are provided, which are designed to develop the many traits identified in the ETS to be necessary for employees to do their job well or to take on new responsibilities.

This system also provides a transparent framework for self-directed career development. It clearly establishes every employee's job role and needed skills, as well as the capabilities they will need in order to move on to other roles or a more senior position; there is no need for second-guessing. The ETS allows individuals to direct their career advancement according to their own aspirations, and yet in a way that is aligned to the company's business needs. They can see for themselves what the company asks for, where new opportunities for advancement lie and what it would take for them to get there. Employees can then focus on developing skills specific to their current roles or explore new skills needed for the roles to which they aspire.

Career Framework

One relatively new enhancement to IBM's expertise management system is our career framework. If the ETS provides a holistic view of the company's total capabilities and where each IBMer stands in relation to the whole, the career framework is a structure that provides guidance, tools and resources to help employees develop expertise over time and, hence, progress in their careers. The idea is to help employees understand the core capabilities that IBM needs to deliver, and what employees need to do to help our clients become successful as business strategies and needs change over time.

At IBM, we regard expertise as defined by many core capabilities that can be leveraged across the business. They are a composite of applied knowledge, trained skills, education and on-the-job experience. In order to develop expertise, IBMers perform designated activities and achieve successful and consistent results that fulfil specified requirements in the framework. By doing so, they reach specific milestones of proficiency, from the basic "Entry" level to the highest "Thought Leader" level. The various capabilities that make up this framework are defined much like major and minor subjects at university. Continual self-assessment, as well as mentoring, formal learning programmes and peer learning are part of the activities in place to support this development process.

The advantage of this career framework is that it allows employees the flexibility to progress along different career trajectories, whether in a linear (e.g., consistent deepening of a specialisation) or non-linear (that is, developing across many careers, resulting in development of multiple capabilities to varying levels) fashion. So our people are able to define and grow their own careers, transferring previously learned skills to new, but related, job roles and expanding their roles within the company.

For example, a consultant at IBM may choose over time to become a general manager instead. The career framework provides avenues by which he can do so, by identifying the learning path he needs to take and the subsequent opportunities within the company on a business or global level. They can also grow to become the acknowledged thought leaders in their specialty.

The career framework also nurtures those employees who have deep proficiency in one field (for instance, engineering), but who can also benefit from some degree of knowledge across different areas of activity (such as marketing, design or finance). These "T-shaped" individuals, who often possess a strong mix of business, technical and people skills and can serve as strong collaborators, innovators and communicators, add to the company's competitive advantage in an evolving global business environment where such versatility is in high demand.

Under the career framework, management roles are just one of the many tracks through which employees can rotate into and out of as they advance. Our philosophy is not to prescribe any fixed path to advancement, but to enable multiple career paths, all of which benefit the company and could potentially lead to executive positions. There is no predefined timeline; the individual determines the pace of progress, in accordance with the evolving business needs of the company and his or her own aspirations and priorities.

Conclusion

IBM's approach to career management and development is a response to major trends and driving forces that continue to shape our global business practice today. What we have today in the ETS and its career framework and development process is a rational, transparent and comprehensive structure for career management across our entire global operation. One of the key challenges of operating as a global company in diverse new markets in the Asia-Pacific is the need to establish a common language, shared values and consistent organisational culture across a large and dynamic geographical expanse. I believe that IBM's flexible yet comprehensive approach is well suited to embrace this challenge.

As a global company, we must continually review and update our framework and expertise to ensure that they are relevant to evolving client needs. This is a never-ending process of continuous improvement in which there is always something to learn: from our business environment and competitors, from our clients, partners and our employees. The IBMer is on the frontlines of modern business practice, and must be equipped with the best possible skills, com-petencies and capbilities in the pursuit of excellence. Our philosophy is to place the IBMer at the heart of a versatile, self-directed career management strategy that can support our dynamic business needs as well as our employees' personal aspirations. As IBM's legendary president Thomas Watson, Jr. reminds us, it is the talent, energy, intelligence and commitment of our people that will be the key to our success.

Reference

Watson, Jr., T.J. (1963). *A Business and Its Beliefs: The Ideas That Helped Build IBM*. New York: McGraw-Hill.

25

The Real Superstars

Robert Sutton

Over the past few years, with the rise of Asia as an economic force, I have been fortunate to run workshops and give speeches for groups from a host of countries from the region including China, India, Singapore, Vietnam and Taiwan. One of the messages I am always careful to emphasise is that, as they work with Western companies and management experts, Asian companies need to be especially careful not to import management philosophies and practices that are widely used, but either have been demonstrated to be ineffective or — although effective under a narrow set of conditions — would not transfer well to most other national and company cultures. I urge them, "Don't make the same stupid mistakes we have made."

In particular, perhaps the most misguided Western management practices are those that glorify solo superstars, especially those systems where people are ranked from worst to best; those placed at the top of the pile have considerable incentive not to cooperate with their peers (who they are competing with) and, in fact, have much incentive to ignore and even undermine their peers because it helps enhance their relative ranking. The glorification of individual superstars is, in most companies, a misguided application of the Western (especially in the US) fascination with rugged and self-sufficient individuals and sports, such as golf and automobile racing, where there is just one individual who is glorified as the winner. The best evidence shows that the application of this mindset to career and incentive systems undermines both individual development and organisational performance (Hansen, 2009; Pfeffer and Sutton, 2006).

To illustrate, the defunct Merrill Lynch (now part of Bank of America) had a pay system and cultural values that glorified solo selfish stars, and that demonstrates the folly of using them when the goal is cooperation and the development of a pool of talented people. In *Riding the Bull*, Paul Stiles (1998) describes his experiences as a new trader in Merrill Lynch. During his first weeks on the job, he asked for help, advice and tips from seasoned traders so he could learn how to do his work as quickly and as effectively as possible. Stiles reports that his new colleagues largely ignored him because their bonuses were based only on individual financial performance. From their perspective, taking time to mentor and train Stiles was at odds with their self-interest — every minute they spent with Stiles costs them money. So there was a strong norm against helping newcomers learn the ropes, which was reinforced by those in senior positions because, after all, they had been promoted because they were selfish stars. As Dan and Chip Heath (2009) tell it,

> "Eventually, Stiles was reduced to silently observing their behavior from a distance, like a rogue MBA anthropologist.

It surely never dawned on the person who set up Merrill Lynch's incentive system that the traders' bonuses would make training new employees impossible."

In contrast to this discouraging story, Morten Hansen's masterful book *Collaboration* shows how organisations that consistently hire, develop and promote "T-shaped" people, those who "simultaneously deliver results on the job" (the vertical part of the "T") *and* deliver results by collaborating across the company (the horizontal part of the "T") typically outperform their rivals independently of other nuances of their reward and promotion systems and culture. Given the Western temptation to overglorify solo superstars, I was pleased to see that at least three of the multinationals represented at our Executive Roundtable had developed such sophisticated and effective systems for developing and promoting T-shaped people. The head of IDEO's Shanghai office, Richard Kelly, explained that this was a strong cultural value in the company and that they used it relentlessly in selecting and evaluating people — they sought and promoted people with deep expertise in areas such as mechanical engineering, industrial design, human factors, operations and business strategy — but that alone was not enough. Successful IDEO consultants also need to have broad technical interests so they can more effectively combine their knowledge with experts, and they need to have social and interpersonal skills so they can interact effectively with both clients and each other.

The essay from General Electric (GE) is fascinating in this regard because the company is so explicit about specifying its definition of a star employee, and so vehement about the damage done by star performers who undermine GE's culture. As the graphic in their essay shows, and researchers who have studied GE observe (e.g., Ulrich et al, 2002), the company sees adherence to collective values (including cooperation, information sharing and mentoring) as just as important as their individual performance. Indeed, GE is especially quick to remove solo stars who defy and undermine company values because it sends a strong message to other employees that senior leadership is not just paying lip service to the importance of values. As GE executives discussed at the Roundtable and note in this volume, the company is considerably more tolerant and optimistic about careers of employees who embrace and enact GE values, but have performance problems. When such cases arise, the company devotes considerable effort to developing the person's skills so he or she can become a top performer, and to finding a different job in the company where his or her strengths can shine through.

The essay from IBM (see Chapter 24) indicates that this large multinational firm is also dedicated to attracting, promoting and developing people with the skills to be star performers and who support, rather than undermine, cultural values of collaboration. The IBM essay emphasises how T-shaped people with a mix of technical, business and interpersonal skills add to the company's competitive advantage, and is at the heart of their approach to career development. IBM also seems to take the notion of T-shaped people a step further, as they discuss the importance of hiring, developing and promoting versatile and flexible employees because it is so difficult to predict what skills will be needed in the future, when they will be needed and where they will be needed. Certainly, as T-shaped people tend to have broader skills and better political and interpersonal skills than pure specialists who never venture outside of their narrow domains, there is good reason to believe that they are better prepared to notice and adjust to new business demands and to realise when it is the right, and the wrong, time to "intelligently apply one's arsenal of competencies and experiences to a broad range of activities, including new and unexpected situations." At IBM, they call such people "Versatilists" and, while I think that term embraces the notion of T-shaped people, there is also an additional set of elements implied. These include tolerance for ambiguity and uncertainty, the ability to quickly mobilise oneself and others when unexpected and pressing threats arise, and the capacity to improvise and experiment with new approaches when it is clear that existing methods and traditions are failing or will fail.

I was quite taken with this emphasis on developing "Versatilists" because so many education systems in the world — especially in Asian countries like China and Japan, but also increasingly in Western countries — do little to teach flexibility, imagination and improvisation. Rather, students learn to memorise the right answers to questions and are taught to perform in a setting where there is always a correct and known answer to every question or challenge, be it an answer on a standardised test or knowing the one "true" answer to the teacher's question. The implication, as IDEO's Kelly suggested, is that the Asian companies he works with (and I would add many Western companies as well) would do well to teach their people methods for doing imaginative work, to instill creative confidence in them and to encourage more playfulness — as it fuels creativity, engagement and good mental health. In IBM's language, I would argue these are all hallmarks for developing successful "Versatilists".

In closing, I am struck by three directions that leaders of Asian companies, especially multinationals that have substantial presence in Asia, seem to be going. These are all generally healthy patterns and I am impressed with both the progress made by the companies at the Roundtable and the directions they are headed. First, there is strong evidence that the once common glorification of solo selfish superstars is disappearing quickly in both Western and Asian companies, especially those with the most sophisticated reward and career development systems. Second, we are in an era where cooperative skills, political savvy and self-awareness are required job skills. Third, imagination, improvisation and innovation will become increasingly important skills.

Yet, I have a couple of nagging worries about the possible unintended negative side effects that leaders of Asian companies ought to guard against. These negative effects stem from the first two trends and have the potential to undermine the third trend towards imagination, improvisation and innovation. My first nagging worry is that there is a risk of emphasising T-shaped people and "Versatilists" too much. The fact is that, if you look at research on expertise, the most skilled people in our society — be they scientists, musicians, poets, athletes or surgeons — are narrow specialists and developed their skills by being hyper-focused on some narrow area for years and years, usually for decades (Gladwell, 2008). We desperately need such specialists, and if they are socially inept or lack general knowledge in other areas, rather than firing or reforming these "I-shaped" people, sometimes a better solution is to team them up with socially adept generalists who could do the job of translating their work and explaining it to others. Indeed, some of the most innovative organisations find ways to team up socially and politically skilled generalists with brilliant specialists who are unable or unwilling to "waste" time selling their ideas or talking to specialists from other domains (Sutton, 2002).

My second nagging worry is that, while I believe that having an organisation that is populated by people who accept and demonstrate an organisation's cultural values and work practices is a hallmark of great companies, there is a risk that such an approach can promote so much conformity and similar world views that badly needed cultural changes cannot occur because, as the old saying goes, "when everyone thinks alike, no one thinks very much." As such, to breed both imagination and the potential for cultural change, wise Asian leaders might develop and protect a few small pockets of constructive deviants, who are charged with questioning the ways that people think and act, and inventing and experimenting with new ways. In this regard, one of the most successful and imaginative organisations in the world is animated filmmaker Pixar. A key juncture in the organisation's history came when executives Steve Jobs, Ed Catmull and John Lasseter hired Brad Bird to direct *The Incredibles* and instructed him to challenge Pixar's status quo. They brought in Bird because they were worried, after three huge successes starting with *Toy Story 1*, that things were going *too well*. The first thing Bird did was to assemble a team of "malcontents" who did not like the way that Pixar did things. The result was a lot of constructive conflict within Bird's team and between his team and others at Pixar. Ultimately, they produced *The Incredibles*, which was a huge financial success and won the Academy Award for the best animated film (Rao et al, 2008).

I am not arguing that the leaders of Asian firms ought to encourage wild insubordination and rebellion against the status quo. That is a quick and painful route to failure. Yet, when used in small doses and with proper precautions, breeding pockets of constructive deviance can interject badly needed creativity and cultural change.

References

Gladwell, M. (2008). *Outliers*. New York: Little, Brown and Company.

Hansen, M.T. (2009). *Collaboration*. Boston: Harvard Business School Press.

Heath, D. and C. Heath. (2009). Why incentives are effective, irresistible, and almost certain to backfire. *Fast Company Magazine*, Issue 132 (February). http://www.fastcompany.com/magazine/132/made-to-stick-curse-of-incentives.html. Accessed on 17 July 2010.

Pfeffer, J. and R.I. Sutton. (2006). *Hard Facts, Dangerous Half-truths, and Total Nonsense*. Boston: Harvard Business School Press.

Rao, H., R.I. Sutton and A.P. Webb. (2008). Innovation lessons from Pixar: an interview with Oscar-winning director Brad Bird. *The McKinsey Quarterly*. http://www.mckinseyquarterly.com/Innovation_lessons_from_Pixar_An_interview_with_Oscar-winning_director_Brad_Bird_2127. Accessed on 17 July 2010.

Stiles, P. (1998). *Riding the Bull*. New York: Random House.

Sutton, R.I. (2002). *Weird Ideas That Work*. New York: Free Press.

Ulrich, D., S. Kerr and R. Ashkenas. (2002). *The GE Work-Out*. New York: McGraw-Hill.

Leaders Who Coach Individuals and Design Organisation Career Processes

Dave Ulrich

L eaders who manage careers attend to both individual and organisation issues. At the individual level, leaders help people (including themselves) make more informed career choices. At the organisation level, leaders establish processes and systems that build a career capability throughout their company. Both individual and organisation career issues deserve increasing leadership attention because the common Asian tradition of a lock-step career, where an employee was predestined for a career track, has been replaced with employees who have the luxury of making choices about their careers (and they are increasingly mobile) in growing Asian organisations.

Individual: Managing the Personal Aspects of a Career

Leaders who attend to the personal dimensions of a career not only help employees make wise career choices, they also demonstrate personal sensitivity to issues that are important to employees. In addition, leaders who manage their own careers are in a position to help employees better manage theirs. There is a large literature on personal career choices (Bolles, 2005, 2009; Lore, 1998), but we have synthesised seven questions that leaders can use to help individuals (including themselves) make better career choices (Ulrich and Ulrich, 2010). As Asian leaders engage in career dialogues with subordinates, new employees, mentees or other employees, they may use the following questions to help employees make more informed career choices.

What Do You Want to be Known For?

Which job, career or life choice will build on your strengths and best match your identity with the organisation brand? How can you express your core values in your daily work? Leaders who help employees recognise their strengths will be more able to help those employees match their strengths with their job, career and organisation. As Asian organisations grow internationally, employees who deal well with uncertainty, have high tolerance for ambiguity and have a high threshold for change will be more likely to succeed in these global assignments.

Where are You Going?

What impact do you want to make on what types of problems? We have distilled the personal goals literature into four drivers that lead to problems employees like to solve:

1. *Insight.* Employees like to work on gaining new ideas and trying new things.
2. *Achievement.* Employees like to see results happen and track their success with visible results.
3. *Relationships.* Employees like to connect with others and be part of a social network.
4. *Empowerment.* Employees like to build sustainable organisations and results.

Asian leaders who help employees identify their personal drivers of success may then steer employees into jobs and careers which match those drivers.

Who Do You Want to Travel With?

Which job, career or life choice will help you build relationships that matter to you? A large part of any employee's career success depends on who they have positive relationships with. Leaders help employees build skills of good relating (e.g., listening, bidding, apologising and problem solving). Leaders also help employees work in settings where their needs for social connections are met. When employees work with people they consider their friends, they are more productive and creative and have higher retention. Employees who are more introverted will work better by themselves than employees who are more extroverted. Asian organisations supplement the strong Asian commitment to families and become an emotional and community support.

How Do You Build a Positive Work Environment?

Which job, career or life choice will be done in a work setting that you personally enjoy? Leaders help shape a work culture that nourishes and encourages employees. They also help align that work culture with the personal styles of employees. A positive work environment is often characterised by clear expectations, extensive communications, openness/transparency and inviting physical space. Leaders help individuals stay connected when the work environment affirms individual employees.

What Challenges Interest You?

Which job, career or life choice will offer you opportunities to do work that is easy, energising and enjoyable for you personally? Leaders can help employees make choices about the type of work they do (intellectual, physical, social), where they work (office versus remote location, inside versus outside, domestic versus global), when they work (flexible versus fixed hours) and the characteristics of the work (innovative versus routine, autonomy versus shared, opportunity for growth versus stability, visibility versus behind the scenes). As leaders help employees make choices about the characteristics of work that work for them, these employees will have better careers.

How Do You Learn from Your Work?

Which job, career or life choice will help you grow, learn and develop resilience when facing change? Leaders help employees learn from career choices. If a job or career choice was successful, leaders probe why and help employees replicate the success. If a job or career choice did not work, leaders help employees learn to adapt to future settings. Employees who learn from their career choices develop resilience and broaden their future career opportunities.

What Delights You?

Which job, career or life choice will bring a sense of joy and delight to your personal and professional life? Leaders help employees find room in their careers for pleasure, playfulness, creativity and living in the moment. When employees are mindful about what they are working for, they are more able to find meaning in their work setting.

Too often, leaders do not talk to their employees about their career and performance for various reasons. Often, they do not want to raise expectations about a specific job, or they do not want to argue about things they cannot control. Just as typically, they do not have a framework and language to talk about career development in a useful way, especially to professional employees. As leaders ask these questions of their employees and of themselves, they enable their employees to make more informed career choices. These questions are timeless and work in both up and down markets to help people find a sense of meaning in their work lives. As Asian organisations grow both through innovative products and services and through global expansion, leaders will need to help employees make more informed career choices. These questions frame a conversation a leader may have with an employee (and with themselves) so that the latter adapts his or her career to evolve with the organisation.

Organisation: Shaping Career Processes in Organisations

While much of the leadership work on careers is done through personal conversations using the above seven questions, the symposium also focused on how leaders build career development systems within their organisations.

251

These leaders build organisation career processes around four questions, and the GE and IBM cases illustrate each of these in an Asian context. Let us highlight how leaders can pay attention to each of these four questions.

1. Why Careers Matter?

Successful multinational companies, such as GE and IBM, have created a strong and simple rationale for investing in career management: organisations that have the capability of helping employees manage their careers will attract better employees, have more productive employees, have the right people in the right positions making the right decisions and, ultimately, increase customer and investor results. As Asian employees have increased choice about where to work, and some Asian countries have high employee mobility, those companies who offer rigorous career management processes will be more attractive to employees to join and to stay. As Asian companies evolve from local to global positioning, they will require employees who have new skills sets. It is interesting that the two case studies of career management come from multinationals doing business in Asia more than local Asian companies.

2. What Skills are Required?

Traditionally, professional employees evolved their career through four stages (Dalton and Thompson, 1986):

1. *Stage 1 (Apprentice).* Employees are dependent, working under the direction of others, helping and learning from more experienced people who may serve as bosses, mentors or coaches. Work is never entirely his or her own, but rather are assignments given that

are portions of a larger project being actively overseen by a more senior professional.

2. *Stage 2 (Individual contributor).* Employees demonstrate their competence as independent contributors and go indepth into one problem or technical area. They develop credibility and a reputation as an expert, and use their burgeoning confidence to develop more of his or her own interior and exterior resources to succeed on the job.

3. *Stage 3 (Manager).* The professional begins to expand beyond his or her technical expertise. This professional manages others through ideas and information, and helps to develop others as an idea leader, mentor, team leader or manager.

4. *Stage 4 (Strategist).* The individual provides direction for the organisation, exercising formal and informal power to initiate action and influence decisions. He or she may represent the organisation inside and outside its boundaries, and is in a position to act as a sponsor for other employees to help prepare them for key roles in the organisation.

Traditional career theory holds that individuals would evolve through these four stages, with increasing responsibility, scale and scope.

Today, the approach to careers has shifted from a linear (four stages) to a "Y" model (see Figure 26.1). In this model, which was validated in the symposium, the first two stages are much the same, as the individual learns what is expected of him or her (stage 1) and develops mastery in a particular area (stage 2). Next, leaders help employees make a significant choice between either a managerial or technical career track. Along the managerial track, employees learn how to manage

Figure 26.1 The "Y" model of career development

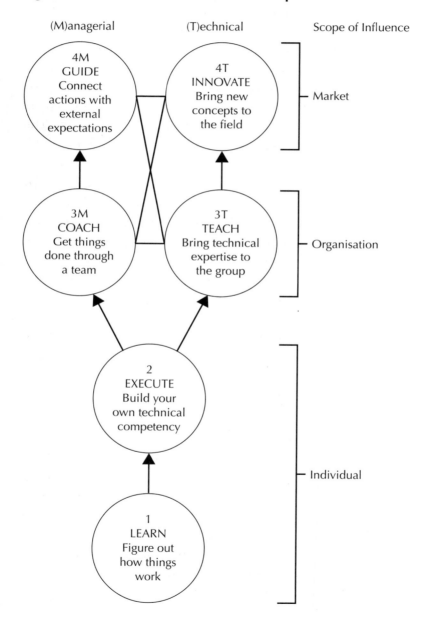

others and get work done through others; along the technical track, employees gain increased specialisation and depth in their target functional domain. Leaders help employees make the career trade-offs, and they also make sure that their organisation has the right mix of individuals in both tracks. If too many individuals go into the managerial track, the organisation becomes more generalist and lacks specialists who have deep technical expertise. If the organisation has too many in the technical track, they may not gain the scale and scope they desire.

These choices are critical for Asian organisations that want to grow. Leaders of these organisations need to help employees make choices about their desire to move up a managerial versus technical career track, and to make sure that their organisations can manage both tracks. Once these tracks are defined, leaders can explicitly define the knowledge, skills and abilities of individuals in each role. These competency models then become the standards for what employees should know and do so that they can move up their desired career track.

3. How to Assess Skills?

Once standards are set based on career paths, leaders can ensure that employees know how they are doing against those standards. Some of this employee awareness may come from regular performance reviews or leadership feedback using tools such as the leadership 360 assessment. Other employee awareness may come from information conversations between a leader and his or her employees so that the latter knows not only what is expected for today's work, but what would be expected to move into desired positions for future work. This formal assessment process may be difficult for some

Asian organisations that rely more on implicit rather than explicit, performance management processes.

4. How to Invest in Building Future Skills?

Finally, leaders help organisations develop career capabilities by offering an integrated approach to employee development. Some responsibility for employee development rests with the employee as the latter self-selects into development assignments and training. However, leaders also have some responsibility to help employees have a regular and rigorous individual development plan that matches an employee's career aspirations to an organisation's investment in development. A career development plan often has three dimensions (see Figure 26.2):

1. *Areas for improvement.* Based on the standards and assessment against standards, the leader and employee identify specific development improvements.
2. *Potential development activities.* The leader, working with the HR Department, can lay out anywhere from ten to 15 possible development activities (see some listed). These are alternative ways an employee can improve his or her skills.
3. *Timing.* The timing might be months or quarters, but they represent a time frame for when the employee can expect to participate in the development activity.

By preparing an individual development plan for each employee, leaders not only help the particular employee become more effective, but they also help build the reputation of a company as one which is concerned about career development.

Figure 26.2 Individual development plan

Employee: (name)
Areas for improvement: (specific goals and improvements required)

-
-
-

Potential Developmental Activity	Time Period						
	1	2	3	4	5	6	Others
Attend external technical training							
Attend external managerial training							
Attend internal training							
Formal job assignment							
Participate in task force							
Be invited to make key presentation							
Participate in or supervise philanthropy work							
Join professional associations							
Become connected through social media							
Be part of task force							
Participate in external leadership positions							
Represent the company to external groups							
Do job sharing with other key jobs							
Visit other companies on site visit							
Participate in regular reading programme							
Do shadow leadership							
Others							

Putting This into a Systemic and Regular Process

GE, IBM and other leading global companies have put these steps into their regular process. This process generally includes a regular time for each step of leadership development. Leaders who organise and work on this process help their company build leadership capability.

Conclusion

Leaders who manage individual career discussions show their concern for employees and help the latter become more aware of their career choices. Leaders who build organisation career systems build the capability and reputation of their organisation which helps attract, retain and engage employees.

References

Bolles, R.N. (2005). *How to Find Your Mission in Life*. New York: Ten Speed Press.

Bolles, R.N. (2009). *What Color is Your Parachute?* New York: Ten Speed Press.

Dalton, G. and P. Thompson. (1986). *Novations: Strategies for Career Management*. Glenview, Illinois: Scott, Foresman and Company.

Lore, N. (1998). *The Pathfinder: How to Choose or Change Your Career for a Lifetime of Satisfaction and Success*. Newport Pagnell, UK: Fireside Books.

Lore, N. (1998). *Now What?* Newport Pagnell, UK: Fireside Books.

Ulrich, D. and W.L. Ulrich. (2010). *The Why of Work*. New York: McGraw-Hill.

PART EIGHT

Generating Leaders

27

In the Company of Leaders: IBM's Approach to Future-ready Leadership Development

Cordelia Chung

As new markets and new demands supersede traditional hinterlands and established business paradigms, it has become even more difficult for companies to predict with any certainty what future success will entail. The challenge has deepened as the pace and range of globalisation continue to increase; content expertise, seniority or local experience alone are no longer sufficient to distinguish the successful leader of the future. In Asia, many established companies are often family-owned, with a strong emphasis on discipline, execution and hard-won expertise. In the new business environment, many of these firms, building on the foresight and energies of their entrepreneurial founders, are looking to a new generation of leadership for the cosmopolitan perspective, management savvy and business acumen they will need in order to transit to, and thrive in, a globalised economy. But effective leaders cannot be nurtured overnight. Any organisation interested in its continual success should regard the ongoing development and renewal of its leadership as a core imperative and key investment over time.

Towards Future-ready Leadership

Leadership has always been understood as a key competitive advantage and defining strength for IBM; this is why leadership development is a purposeful and broad-based process that constantly evolves with changing business needs. *Fortune* magazine, ranking IBM as Number One in its list of Top Companies for Leaders in 2009, highlighted the rigour, range and innovation of our practices, which have also translated into outstanding business results to match.

As a large, global company operating in rapidly changing sectors, IBM embraces a broad and wide-ranging concept of leadership. The divergent, diverse economic landscape in which we do business means that it is not sufficient for superior performance to be left to a select few stars, or to those appointed to executive positions. Instead, success depends on being able to attract, develop and mobilise a versatile pool of talent that is more likely to spot, seize and make the most of new opportunities as they arise from an evolving economic landscape. Every employee, regardless of position or job role, should be able to proactively identify and take responsibility for what needs to be done, to do so in a timely manner and in alignment with corporate objectives. Everyone in the firm must create the conditions in which the company can succeed.

"IBM at Its Best": Identifying Leadership Competencies

Central to IBM's strategy is the careful identification and cultivation of nine leadership competencies — key performance behaviours validated through deep research, business practice and the foresight of senior company leaders — that demonstrate how successful leaders act when they are at their best:

1. *They embrace challenge and take charge.* In a company engaged with complex situations, from daily breakthroughs to world-changing progress, successful leaders are future-oriented and embrace hard challenges that confront their teams, clients and communities. The leader takes personal accountability for transformative outcomes. They find and seize opportunity in the midst of complexity, identifying central issues and charting effective solutions.

2. *They form effective partnerships.* The successful leader takes time to form effective connections with partners across the whole company as well as outside the company, working alongside clients to co-create mutual success and transformative outcomes.

3. *They collaborate globally.* Being a globally integrated company is about becoming global professionals and global citizens. This means thinking and working across boundaries of teams, disciplines, organisations, countries and cultures. Collaborative skills are a must, as is the ability to tap on the collective intelligence of personal, business and company networks as well as engendering collective action to achieve shared goals.

4. *They are systems thinkers.* The leader helps clients, colleagues and other partners to see an end-to-end view of issues from many different angles, allowing bold and appropriate action to be taken with a fuller understanding of relevant data, underlying patterns and significant parameters.

5. *They build mutual trust.* The leader brings different constituents together to solve problems and open up opportunity. This requires skill at finding common ground for those with different objectives, aspirations, constraints and cultures. Building "360 degrees of trust" means building positive relationships with integrity and openness across all groups of stakeholders.

6. *They influence through expertise.* Leaders conscientiously deepen their own and their colleagues' knowledge and eminence — as professionals, collaborators and experts.

7. *They are intellectually curious, open-minded and inclusive.* In a world where the future is far less predictable, the leader must actively seek what is not yet known or imagined, be open to new ideas and approaches, and rethink assumptions. This also means engaging others whose backgrounds, cultures, languages or work styles are different in order to learn, adapt and seek constructive transformation.

8. *They communicate for impact.* The leader listens to find mutual understanding and then communicates to build a sense of shared outcomes, grounded in deep expertise, perspective and judgement. Faced with complex or even unpopular situations, the leader puts a point across clearly, simply and

authentically, balancing disparate concepts, strategies and goals in the most timely, transparent and effective manner.

9. *They serve the success of others.* Leadership is about bringing one's best self to work in the service of the success of others. This is as much about anticipating and removing obstacles to progress, as it is about providing timely and relevant input, resources and support. The leader helps colleagues and partners learn and enhance their own capability to succeed, creating an environment in which fellow stakeholders feel a sense of purpose and engagement, and in which they are most motivated by their own desire to act.

These leadership competencies are not specific to a management track, nor any division of business, but cut across all aspects of the company. They describe what best distinguishes IBM employees in our interaction with clients and with each other. This means that leaders may emerge from anywhere in the company, and expectations of successful business values and behaviour are applied to all employees at every level. Every IBMer is regarded, and expected to act, as a potential leader.

Another characteristic of IBM's development approach is that there is no set path or time frame to senior leadership positions. Instead, successful leaders at IBM are those who are best able to take ownership for the success of the company by perfecting these success-oriented behaviours, regardless of which aspect of the company's business they are involved in. The IBM leader is the embodiment of IBM at its best.

Nurturing Leaders in IBM ASEAN

In IBM ASEAN, identified high performance employees are systematically groomed to become future leaders in the company's ASEAN Leadership Group, under the sponsorship of the General Manager and members of the Leadership Group. Known as the ASEAN Leadership Team (ALT), this promising community of 86 leaders from across all countries and business units in IBM ASEAN spend 18 months in developmental activities that prepare them to take on responsibilities as the next wave of senior leadership in the region.

To identify this next generation of leaders, different critical job roles are carefully outlined and mapped, along with key performance measures (such as revenue, growth, profit or client satisfaction), the core capabilities needed to do the job well, and the competencies aligned with each job function. These are measured against the current pool of IBMers to ascertain how many employees are ready to take on each critical job role. Should there be a shortfall in the pipeline (e.g., there are not enough IBMers whose career paths will prepare them to take on a Country General Manager role), targeted interventions can be put into place.

Apart from functional capabilities acquired through current functional roles and job rotation, leadership development for the ALT also entails a framework of programmes designed to develop the Leadership Competencies, Business and Strategic Acumen, and Strategic Networks of these high potential employees. A Leadership Framework Survey benchmarks them against key leadership traits, revealing any gaps or corrective action to be taken. This also helps to address potential derailment risks early; for instance, if otherwise competent managers lack communication or consensus-building competencies, these can be addressed transparently and relatively early in their careers. The LEADing@IBM programme and Learning Suites support leadership competencies with an action learning framework. Strategic business acumen is developed through formal core courses leading to certification, including the eCornell Business Leadership programme, and further enhanced through special challenge assignments.

An important aspect of leadership development at IBM involves opportunities for IBMers to connect and network with a diverse range of contacts both across and beyond the company. This is facilitated through a range of certified electives, participation in broad business leadership programmes, as well as formal and informal collaboration and strategic networking opportunities designed to enhance cross-boundary interaction and teaming skills. IBM's Global Citizen's Portfolio also provides a series of programmes for IBMers to deepen their partnerships with the company in support of their education, skills building and personal development. We also actively nurture mentoring (both receiving and learning to provide mentorship) as a means to facilitate the inter-generational transfer of knowledge and to encourage a corporate culture of leaders as teachers.

IBM's Corporate Service Corps

One important component under IBM's Global Citizen's Portfolio is the Corporate Service Corps (CSC), an "outside the classroom" immersion programme that *Fortune* magazine has highlighted as a forward-thinking and proactive aspect of IBM's leadership development strategy. Launched in July 2008, the CSC receives thousands of applications worldwide, and has already deployed over 700 IBM employees from 47 countries on 70 teams to Brazil, China, Egypt, India, Ghana, Malaysia, Nigeria, the Philippines, Poland, Romania,

South Africa, Tanzania, Turkey and Vietnam. As of May 2010, 19 ASEAN participants have completed their CSC assignments and nine more have been confirmed, including one from Singapore.

Participants form multinational, multidisciplinary teams of eight to 15 people support the efforts of non-governmental organisations, public agencies, local entrepreneurs and educational institutions for up to six months. IBMers with high potential are involved directly in tackling community-driven economic development projects at the intersection of business, technology, society and corporate social responsibility. They contribute their passion and expertise to projects that expose them to all the key elements of 21st century business: emerging markets, diverse cultures, global teaming, complex policy environments, cross-functional collaboration, increasing societal expectations and game-changing solutions. A multilayered, hands-on leadership learning experience with cascading benefits, the CSC programme has captured the imagination of IBMers around the world.

Let me illustrate with an example. In Vietnam, the IBM team partnered with the local People's Committee to develop a game plan for urban development in Ho Chi Minh City, covering key areas such as food safety, water management, transportation and growing a high-tech ecosystem. The team researched best practices in other countries, consulted IBM experts in each of the focus areas, and presented recommendations for pilot programmes in collaboration with city experts and officials. In doing so, they helped the city to understand and plan their urban infrastructure as one fully interconnected, interdependent system for the first time.

For IBM, CSC is more than just a developmental programme; by sharpening our best new minds in addressing real issues with effective solutions around the world, we are also reaffirming our commitment as a corporation to shaping a better world and staying relevant to the most pressing concerns of our time.

Diversity in IBM

In a region marked by a tremendous spectrum of different cultures and societies, IBM's long history of commitment to diversity and equal opportunity has been both a proud tradition and an extraordinary competitive business advantage. Indeed, DiversityInc named IBM the Number One company for global diversity in 2010. This core corporate philosophy of embracing diversity and non-discriminatory practices has helped IBM ASEAN to leverage the best possible ideas, talent and results in the region, regardless of race, gender, language or creed. Over 30 nationalities now work in IBM ASEAN; over one third of the executive staff are women. The same proportion is reflected in the pipeline of future leaders. In a complex and ever-changing global business environment, actively building a diverse team makes sense; it helps us better understand markets, unlock synergies and unleash innovation. IBM ASEAN's diversity represents a wealth of perspectives that is reflected in the Leadership Team's composition, strengthening its effectiveness and adaptability as a regional and international business team.

For this reason, a successful leader in the IBM ASEAN team is also an acknowledged and valuable leader anywhere in the world. Our people have certainly demonstrated their quality well beyond their home region. Three former General

Managers of IBM Singapore, all Singaporeans, have moved on to executive positions outside ASEAN: Ong Hoon Meng, who was appointed ASEAN GM in 2007, has also held positions as a Vice-President in IBM Corporate New York and now manages General Business in the Growth Market Unit; Janet Ang and Patricia Yim now hold strategic Vice-President appointments in IBM Greater China after a series of international assignments across different business units, and they also serve on the boards of public councils and panels in Singapore by contributing their leadership and experience to the country's social and economic well-being.

Conclusion

At IBM, we believe that leadership development is self-directed and not predetermined; it is guided by the company's evolving business needs as well as its core values. There should be no discriminatory or other hidden barriers to leadership development. Indeed, diversity should be actively embraced as a competitive strength in today's complex marketplace. Yet, standards must be kept consistent with the company's highest professional and corporate ideals. We harness the passion, initiative, intelligence and expertise of our employees towards challenging, meaningful goals that also support each individual's career aspirations, aligned with corporate and societal outcomes. This layered blend of formal and informal strategies nurtures the successive generations of quality leaders for which IBM is known.

Over a century of experience in the company of leaders has taught us that the path to leadership should take aspirants out of their comfort zones and test their mettle in a broad variety of contexts; leadership cannot be assigned or predetermined in advance, but arises from among those most prepared to embrace challenge, confront the unexpected, harvest the wealth inherent in diversity and make the best of opportunity anywhere, knowing that tomorrow is unlikely to be the same as today. The learnings are clear: leadership can come from anywhere within the company, but it cannot be left to chance. Companies in Asia should provide continual opportunities for its future leaders — and indeed, all capable employees, whatever their backgrounds — to discover and sharpen the key qualities that will give them the best chances of success in the uncharted waters of the 21st century global economy.

28

Developing Leaders in Asia

Deb Henretta

When I came to Asia in 2006, I was amazed by the phenomenal diversity of this continent. I was thrilled to have the opportunity to experience the richness of the region and its vibrant cultures, each bursting with colour and life and yet unique in their history and their expression.

This combination of diversity and uniqueness was not only manifested in what I saw outside, but equally what I saw inside my organisation. More than 75% of our leadership throughout Asia is local and represents the unique talent and cultures of the diverse peoples of the region. And it is the combined strength of this diverse leadership that has allowed Proctor & Gamble (P&G) to rapidly establish itself as one of the leading fast moving consumer goods companies across Asia. Today, we are a multibillion-dollar company reaching out to two billion Asian consumers across 32 countries.

So how do we actively look for, and build leaders who can drive our business across a vast region, inspire people of different ethnicities, languages and temperaments to contribute to building brands and serving consumers better than our competitors?

Leadership Development is a key strategic process in P&G. It is well known that we are a "Build from Within" company. That means, as a policy, we hire talent at the entry level and grow our future leaders internally. We choose not to hire talent directly for leadership levels.

And it is this determination to *grow* leaders that defines our leadership development philosophy. We bring this philosophy to life by embracing a very rigorous tradition and systemic approach to attracting, developing and retaining the finest talent in P&G. It has been the foundation on which we have been able to develop inspirational leaders for more than 172 years.

Attracting the Best Talent

Our first priority is to build a strong foundation by ensuring that the best and the brightest minds across Asia — in China, in Japan, in India, in Australia, in the Philippines, in Indonesia, in Vietnam, in every country where we are present — see P&G as an organisation they would like to work for. Fortunately, our culture and company track record have made us an employer of choice in the vast majority of the communities in which we operate. Across campuses, students look to P&G for careers that ignite their potential by offering opportunities to work on meaningful, real-world projects from the very beginning. They see P&G as a company with diverse, inclusive culture that fosters innovation. They believe that P&G is powered by an exceptional set of people with a broad range of personal attributes and characteristics. All of these further attract the top talent across universities. Every year, P&G receives more than half a million applications from around the globe. In Asia alone, this past year, we received more than 130,000 applications for management positions.

From these applicants, we select those who meet our criteria for success based on a robust behavioural assessment system called "Success Drivers". These analyse their potential to lead, innovate, act decisively, embrace change and so on. Our Success Drivers use cognitive and other tests to map potential recruits onto a Competence Model. Of the hundred thousands of applications in Asia, we hired less than 1% of those applications.

This 1% is, of course, top talent. Our pool primarily comprises students from the finest management schools across Asia, such as Beijing University in China, the Indian Institutes of Management and the National University of Singapore. But beyond being top academic performers, they are also individuals who are looking for careers with companies which do more than just sell products. They are looking for companies that offer more than just a job — those that can provide a meaningful career. A company with a long-term vision that goes beyond profit.

In other words, these are the people with the most potential to lead P&G's Purpose to touch and improve lives, now and for generations to come. Among them are future leaders who will fully realise P&G's growth strategy.

P&G's growth strategy is inspired by our Purpose and is geared to touch and improve the lives of more consumers in more parts of the world more completely. It follows that our growth in Asia will be directly proportionate to how effectively we touch and improve the lives of more consumers in more parts of Asia more completely.

Attracting and then successfully recruiting from among this fine set of potential leaders marks the first step in our Leadership Development Approach.

Develop Top Talent

Once on board, P&G invests significant resources in developing employees and growing top talent into future company leaders. We focus on building their skills and capabilities, providing them with challenging experiences and assignments, and then hot housing high potential talents for accelerated development.

We have institutionalised a comprehensive model of Training and Development that grooms each individual to the best of his or her potential.

We foster a learning culture where leaders teach leaders at all levels of the company. A unique aspect of our training and development programme is the engagement of the senior leadership as trainers to teach future leaders of the company. For example, at our Asia "Senior" Leadership Development College, my top Asian leaders and I serve as the faculty. We are also involved in various ways in other leadership experiences and training for aspiring leaders at the more junior levels in Asia. Our training programmes are customised to the experience level and specific assignments of our employees so they can continue to build their personal capacity and capabilities as they gain experience and assume new roles.

As we do this, we focus on three things: skill development, challenging experiences and accelerated development of high potentials.

On skill development, aside from the fundamental leadership capabilities in strategic thinking and business management, we also focus on critical and uniquely Asian capability needs. These are related to the effectiveness of Asian leaders to lead the diverse, multicultural teams within Asia and influence their global counterparts outside Asia.

More than any other part of the world, leaders in Asia have to constantly adapt their leadership style to inspire and motivate each of the diverse cultures and countries that comprise Asia. Using a single leadership style will prove insufficient given the differences in culture, motivations, rewards and definitions of success in the different countries. Only leaders who can understand and adapt to these local cultures will grow into truly successful pan-Asia leaders. P&G, working with the right external partner, has established a multicultural programme that equips our Asian leaders with deep understanding of how cultures work in a business context and, equally importantly, with skills to "style switch" as they interact with employees from different cultural backgrounds. For example, a Japanese leader will need to adapt to a more direct style as he/she interacts with an Australian manager and then return to a more indirect style when interacting with a Thai peer.

A second focus area for developing our talent is to provide challenging, yet rewarding, on-the-job experiences. P&G plans for these experiences through robust, purposeful succession planning and identification of critical leadership positions across Asia. These experiences broaden exposure to the multicultural setup outside the home country and provide valuable insights into the complexities of leading in Asia. Depending on the needs of the individuals, we also assign cultural mentors who can help facilitate development. We also have robust Assignment Planning and Succession Planning systems which ensure that future leaders have adequate exposure to and experience of different roles and responsibilities that cut across brands, product categories, countries and organisational divisions.

The third focus area within this development step is the identification of high potential individuals early in their career with internally developed High Potential (HiPo) Assessment. The top talent development process will provide accelerated experiences to fast track the growth of those high potential talents we select to grow into the future leaders of our company.

Investments in these three focus areas for employee training and development is a continuous and career-long activity at P&G.

Retain Best Talent

The final step in our leadership development approach is to ensure that we retain our carefully chosen talent, particularly our best leaders. Our company's "Build from Within" policy mandates that we develop and retain talent from the moment we hire them through to their inclusion in our leadership ranks. To do this, we place an enormous emphasis on what we call our Employee Value Proposition or EVP. The EVP is our way of keeping ahead of employee needs and aspirations so we are able to provide a fulfilling work experience at all stages of their careers.

The current EVP centres on our six promises to employees, including:

1. Pride in Company
2. Meaningful Work and Career
3. Healthy Relationship with Manager
4. Learning and Development
5. Competitive and Fair Reward
6. Work-Life Effectiveness

We regularly track our progress against these six areas as well as overall employee satisfaction in an annual employee survey to keep our fingers on the pulse of the organisation, and to help us identify where changes need to be made to keep our proposition current and competitive such that we are able to retain our best talents for the long term.

Asian Leaders For Asia and For the World

P&G's rigorous leadership development programme yields three significant outcomes. First, all critical roles are filled by experienced employees who have demonstrated superior performance in previous assignments and have shown great potential for building both the business and the organisation.

A second outcome is the creation of a diverse Asia organisation and leadership team that reflects the diversity of the consumers we serve. This helps us better understand and respond to our consumer needs and enables more "in-touch" decision making. I am proud to say that P&G's Asia leadership team is recognised as one of the most diverse teams in P&G, both from a gender and nationalities perspective.

Finally, our leadership development efforts produce multidisciplinary leaders with capabilities needed to succeed today and in the future. Members of our leadership team have broad experiences across a variety of P&G business, organisations and functions. They have both breadth and depth of experiences. They can see the strategic big picture, but can also engage in the more operational aspects of the business. And importantly, they have capabilities to successfully work within Asia as well as outside of Asia. We have multiple examples of Asian leaders who are in global roles, such as CEO (P&G UK), Global Innovation Leader (Babycare) and Vice President (Home Care), amongst others. They are all leaders not just for P&G Asia, but for P&G globally.

The future of P&G depends on our investment in leadership development today. We take great pride in the processes and polices that we have developed to help us attract the best talent, develop the skills and capabilities of our top talent and retain that talent over the long term.

But, above all, we take pride in our Purpose of touching and improving lives, now and for generations to come. It is our Purpose that makes this leadership development process comes alive in leaders who inspire our people and develop the next generation of leaders who will help us improve the lives of more consumers in more parts of Asia more completely.

Asia is teeming with top talents who just need the opportunity and the training to develop their leadership skills and capabilities. At P&G, we are happy to have the opportunity to help grow these future leaders for Asia and the globe.

29

Leadership Transition

Michael Jenkins

The Principles

Ensuring a solid leadership pipeline is arguably one of the most pressing issues facing companies and organisations in the Asia-Pacific today. The challenge is a multifaceted one: how do we identify the leaders of tomorrow from the ranks of the people we see today? How do we nurture them and ensure the smooth transition of these gifted people into leadership positions? How do we ensure that we have our fingers on the pulse in terms of understanding whether the leadership needs of the organisation currently are the ones of the future (when in all likelihood, they are not)? What impact will leadership surplus or deficit have on our planning? And yet, these are not the only leadership dilemmas facing organisations in the region; there are a number of other issues that require addressing. Here are some that exercise CEOs and executive teams on a persistent basis:

1. *Alignment to strategy*
   - Our activities around the leadership transition and talent management seem very reactive and disparate: should we not have a clearly defined approach, namely, a formal talent architecture?
   - Will we have only a fast track approach or will we opt more for a "slow burn", that is, to develop people more gradually? How will business needs and the fast changing, macro-economic environment condition drive our decisions on these approaches?
2. *Ownership: who is responsible for leadership?*
   - Who should drive this approach: HR or the business?
   - Will the focus be on managers nominating people as future leaders or will we encourage individuals to put themselves forward?
3. *Targeting*
   - Is our approach to be for specific individuals or are we more concerned with developing capacity? As we manage the leadership transition, is it for the few or for the many?
   - Are we talking about primarily young people, or should we not also consider the dimension represented by an ageing workforce?
4. *Process*
   - How transparent do we want to be around managing the leadership transition? Are we making ourselves vulnerable to accusations of secrecy?
   - To what extent will the needs of the individual be taken into account? Is it only ever about the needs of the organisation?

- Do we expect individuals to take responsibility for managing their own careers, or do we wish it to be entirely organisation-managed?

And last, but not least, is our leadership transition and talent management strategy intended to be about retaining people, or is it more about keeping business critical knowledge in the organisation? Or is it both?

Clearly, there are no straightforward answers to these dilemmas. Indeed, there is no right or wrong way to address them, but there are definitely approaches that are well suited to the size, type, culture and people of individual organisations. These approaches can be adopted and adapted to great effect. Naturally, what works in one context may not be right for another. Nonetheless, there are some useful questions that leaders can ask themselves as well as some valuable lessons to be learned from other organisations. The trick seems to be figuring out what is right for your own organisation as it goes about its own business in its own specific environment. This is achieved by looking at what others have done or are doing, adapting this experience to one's own organisation, and trying things out in the spirit of learning and experimentation. Most companies have reported a process of trial and error: introduction, trialling, evaluation and modification. We would all like to get things right the first time, but in practice the nature of the beast makes it hard to do this.

Implications For Asian Leaders

The implications for Asian leaders are immediate and undoubtedly business critical. One Chinese CEO, an entrepreneur running an 80-strong organisation in Beijing, once shared the following philosophy:

"I don't see what is so difficult about managing the leadership transition. All you have to do is identify the top performers, tell them what you want from them and manage them closely. If they hit their targets, they get to stay. If they don't, they get shown the door. And you just hire in other people who *can* do the job."

Such an approach would surprise many people and yet it is alarmingly prevalent in many companies in Asia.

Many organisations have yet to realise the implications (on costs, morale and engagement) that the lack of a clearly defined leadership transition strategy will have. In India, while Indian universities graduate hundreds of thousands of engineers every year, most companies will confess to finding only a relatively small proportion of these people "viable"; technically, they are competent but managerially, they are wanting. So having found and developed these valuable individuals, it follows that we must do all we can to retain them for as long as we can — certainly for as long as their aspirations and the needs of the company are in alignment.

We also need to consider the type or types of leaders we need to have to take the organisation into the next phase of its development. Much work has been done on understanding how to do this: learning what others have done and considering the applicability of the approach to one's own organisation is the name of the game. Some pointers might include the following for all organisations:

1. *Identifying leadership requirements.* Using leadership competency models to support the selection of new leaders, to help with performance appraisals (necessary for discerning who has what it takes to go to the next leadership level) and also to help form the foundation for leadership development programmes.

2. *Consider the value of diversity.* Asian companies will need to ensure that the top teams of the future are truly representative of the geographies within which the company operates. They will need to look in every corner of the organisation for the talent that will make the difference. Diversity at the top will enable the leadership to be nimble, in tune with the shifting demographics of its customer base and fair.

3. *Leadership development.* Leadership development programmes must form part of the strategy for managing the leadership transition in companies. There is an enormous amount of creativity and flexibility around leadership development programmes in the world today. They include in-classroom experience (through reflection on 360s and other psychometric tools together with peer feedback activities), action learning projects which unfold over weeks or months, having a coach, being coached as part of a team, being mentored by a senior leader and studying for formal qualifications. Forward-looking companies, such as Samsung in Korea, have created fantastic systems for online learning, self-assessment and ongoing leadership development support that meet organisational requirements while simultaneously meeting the development needs of the individual. Some professionals regard online leadership development as lacking in effectiveness because of the lack of in-person interaction. Once again, there is no right answer, but perhaps the challenge is to decide the balance between in-person and online working. We can expect the advance of social networking to have more and more impact in this arena.

4. *Learning by doing.* Research from around the world
   shows that nothing can beat learning leadership
   lessons "on the job". Some argue that this is really
   the only thing that truly counts — and in this era of
   tumultuous change across the region, the acceleration
   in terms of complexity in our world and the ongoing
   challenges brought by ambiguity and in many
   countries and markets, sheer chaos — means that
   old-style, chalk-and-talk approaches to leadership
   development may become increasingly redundant
   unless they can be kept cutting edge, relevant and
   connected to the other methods mentioned above that
   help develop leaders.

For Asian companies whose remit is pan-Asian or global,
other methodologies such as overseas assignments can be
hugely rewarding for the organisation and the individual
alike. In addition to classic expatriation for a certain period
(typically three-year assignments as well as assignments
measured in units of several months), companies can also
consider "in-patriation" assignments whereby personnel
from the outer reaches of the organisation (located away
from the headquarters) can be brought to the headquarters
for exposure to decision makers and counterparts there. This
enables valuable talent to be seen firsthand by top leaders
in the mothership and ensures that the organisation has the
best visibility of the top talent available in the system in
its entirety.

At IBM, we can see how the company has thrown the net
wide in terms of seeking talent not only from Asia, but from
across the globe. The organisation has embraced the concept
of leadership competencies and created a broad-based talent
architecture which is very clear on the kind of leaders

and leadership attributes it is looking for. IBM categorises developmental needs through its ALT Development Plan and seeks to shape its leaders via three key areas: demonstration of key leadership competencies, demonstration of business and strategic acumen, and demonstration of the ability to develop and nurture critical social networks. This last area reflects beautifully the deep need in many parts of the Asia-Pacific for the establishment of strong, durable and long-term human relationships (in contrast to the rather more transactional nature of relationships often noticed in non-Asian contexts). At IBM, there seems to be great enthusiasm for those who are willing to seize opportunities: the self-starter and creative, entrepreneurial leader is a clear winner for IBM. At the same time, the company notes that there will continue to be challenges around true mobility of IBM leaders within Asia itself, that is, the willingness of people to leave the comfort zone of their own country and work in a foreign land where the social mores, language and culture are different.

At P&G, we see great importance attached to the ability of leaders to adapt behaviour to suit a different cultural environment. This "switching" ability is something that other companies and organisations would do well to note, and perhaps emulate, as an example of best practice: those leaders who can switch from a Skype call with Korean colleagues to a difficult conversation with someone in another part of Asia to calling a meeting in Singapore with a team of colleagues from more than 20 different nationalities — and to be able to move seamlessly and seemingly effortlessly from one scenario to the next — is truly a competence that is, and will continue to be, in great demand in the Asia-Pacific.

Broad Lessons Learned

It is clear that managing the leadership transition is not just about the individual. It is about ensuring the long-term management and organisational capability of the organisation. As regards the behaviours and capabilities of leaders, we can ponder the following:

1. *Strategic alignment*
   - Do our potential leaders for tomorrow have a global mindset? Do they understand the world? Can they balance local needs with global ones? Are they curious and interested in learning about people from other countries? Do they have the capability to think strategically across boundaries of culture, time and language? Are they born networkers?
   - Are they astute in terms of understanding the expectations of stakeholders, both local and (as appropriate) global? Are they regarded as good ambassadors for the organisation?
2. *Identification of the right potential leaders*
   - Are they self-aware? Do they encourage diversity of opinion? Are they able to think in a culturally sensitive way?
   - Can they balance control with empowerment? Do they possess the flexibility to know when to intervene and when to let go?
   - Are they excellent communicators? Successful organisations have to be clear not only about their vision and mission, but critically about their *purpose*. Can our future leaders articulate the purpose of the organisation and excite people to action?

- Dealing with ambiguity and uncertainty: can they make bold choices? Are they prepared to take risks? When a crisis arises, can they deal with it effectively?
- Are the future leaders of Asia people who demonstrate integrity and ethical behaviour?

Future Leadership Challenges

Asia stands at the threshold of a thrilling period of growth and discovery. Leaders in Asia have an opportunity to push the frontiers, figuratively and actually, in terms of how we deal with leadership transition. There is evidence that in the Asia-Pacific, home-grown and multinational companies alike have travelled successfully to date along their own individual talent management journeys and, encouragingly for all of us, continue to be open-minded and welcoming of new ideas to strengthen and invigorate their thinking around leadership development.

There is a growing desire to broaden talent pools, promote diversity and open up more career opportunities. We see silos being broken down and a much more mobile set of people, though at the same time, given the cultural background of certain countries, we need to recognise that such mobility demands a great deal of the individual and comes at a price. It is not the same attitude to mobility that we see in other parts of the world.

For example, imagine the agony of the Taiwanese manager who cannot decide between staying on to work in one city, Kaohsiung, where he can simultaneously care for his octogenarian parents and life-long inhabitants of the southern Taiwanese port city, and moving to the capital Taipei to an even more responsible position — but not being able to move his parents whose health he fears will not stand the move which his non-Taiwanese boss says he must make in order to progress? Such human stories will continue to challenge us.

Finally, many organisations are experimenting with the creation of learning environments to foster their leaders' development as leaders through social networks and communities of practice. These initiatives promote leadership practice and development, and help to push leadership transition to the top of the agenda where, given the explosive growth we are witnessing in Asia, it needs to be.

Epilogue

... and Prologue For the Future

30

Essentials of Excellence

Robert Sutton
Dave Ulrich

This book began as a Roundtable discussion and focus group in Singapore among CEOs, Chief Human Resources Officers (CHROs) and thought leaders about the challenges and opportunities of leadership in Asia. There were diverse and often conflicting perspectives expressed throughout these two intensive days. Those of us who participated in these exchanges endured disconcerting stretches, where we struggled to emerge from the fog of confusion that comes with tackling such a broad and vexing topic. Fortunately, as we listened to each other's stories, practices, philosophies, frameworks and evidence, the fog began to clear a bit and we agreed that four questions and eight factors were especially crucial to being a successful leader in Asian companies — be it those that operate primarily in Asia as state-owned enterprises, Western multinationals that have a presence in Asia, or Asian multinationals that have a presence in multiple Asian and Western countries. Chapter 1 lists and explains these institutional and organisational factors. Of course, no framework can capture every nuance of great leadership. But we found this set to be useful both for guiding conversation during the Roundtable and organising the ideas, evidence, cases and stories in this book. Recall that these four questions and eight leadership factors are:

Question	Leadership Success Factor
1. Where are we going?	1. Creating customer-centric actions 2. Implementing strategy
2. How do we get there?	3. Getting past the past 4. Governing through decision making
3. What is work like when we get there?	5. Inspiring collective meaning making 6. Capitalising on capability
4. Who stays and who goes?	7. Developing careers 8. Generating leaders

We believe that these questions and factors serve as a useful checklist for any leader, be they working in or out of Asia, at the top or bottom of an organisation, in a public or private organisation, or a large or small organisation. By answering these questions and taking the subsequent actions, an effective leader devotes attention to a crucial set of institutional and organisational processes. If you, as a leader, only focus on a few of these factors and have not delegated the remaining factors to skilled and trusted colleagues, the chapters here imply that these blind spots will eventually pose a profound risk to your company. We also believe that — although imperfect and incomplete —

the practices, theory and evidence presented in the prior chapters help leaders better understand how to frame these challenges and act effectively to resolve them.

In preparing this final chapter, we reflected on the journey required to complete this book: getting ready for the Roundtable, the challenge and excitement of facilitating it, the numerous exchanges with executives and thought leaders via emails and phone calls, reading and editing their contributions, and writing our own. This process turned our attention to how crucial a leader's personal beliefs, ideas, skills and actions are for turning these success factors into reality, day after day. Indeed, when we say that MediaCorp, DBS and Far East Organization "did" something, that is shorthand for the actions of the individual leaders and followers who populate these companies. Leadership is often about institutional practices around setting strategies, understanding customers, creating purpose, managing careers and so forth, but it is also about having personal capacity and resolve to lead. This insight provoked us to end this volume with a stronger focus on the more personal, and interpersonal, elements of leadership. After all, the best leaders do not just go through the motions of leadership linked to the eight success factors; these actions are propelled by their strong personal conviction, commitment, values and enthusiasm.

This brings us to the question that was used to frame this final chapter: if you were a veteran leader in Asia, what would be the most important advice you could give to a new leader? Of course, every current or aspiring leader who reads this book can and should generate their own answers to this question. We selected five "essentials of excellence" that struck us as especially powerful and useful advice for future leaders in Asia.

1. Explain Your Goals, Values and Strategies in the Simplest Possible Language

One of the most striking things about the CEOs and CHROs at the Roundtable was that they were so remarkably adept at explaining, both to people inside their companies and outside their companies, what they were doing, why they were doing it and where they wanted their organisations to go in simple, actionable language. This is not something that a new leader can do instantly.

We have found it useful to teach new managers about the journey towards true understanding and expertise spelled out by psychologist Will Schutz (1979). He argued that the journey requires travelling through three stages: over-simplification, convoluted confusion and, finally, if a person is persistent enough, profound simplicity. Many times, new and inexperienced leaders believe that they already know, or will quickly discover, the simple truths required to master the craft of leadership. Novices often do not know what they do not know. As a result, after a year or less on the job, the challenges, surprises and complexities often cause rookie leaders to feel overwhelmed. As their experience grows, however, and if they are persistent and mentored properly, they develop a simple and powerful way of understanding who they are, what they are trying to accomplish, and how to explain it in easily understood and actionable language to others.

Being able to explain one's leadership point of view to others means starting with oneself. Effective leaders of others lead themselves by answering questions such as: what is my identity as leader?; what are the strengths I bring to my leadership opportunities and challenges?; what do I want to be known for as a leader?; what do I want to accomplish through my leadership role?; and how can I use my strengths to strengthen those I lead? These self-assessment questions encourage leaders to figure out who they are so that they can better help others become who they need to become. With this personal grounding, leaders are then more able to simplify and communicate their organisation's leadership stories.

Consider just a few examples from the leaders who contributed to this volume. MediaCorp's CEO Lucas Chow's description of a strategic shift from "a national broadcaster to that of a content creator" sounds almost absurdly simple. But these simple words reflected and guided hundreds of large and small changes at MediaCorp that are catalogued in his two pieces in this volume: from eliminating silos to providing the same training to everyone in the company. His personal identity of creating new content is mirrored in his organisation's vision of content creation. Similarly, the essay from GE suggests the simple idea of candid feedback. It also shows us how this is not just hollow rhetoric. Rather, candid feedback is a cornerstone of how GE develops leaders. One consequence of living this simple value is that, when necessary, GE executives make it clear to individuals when and why they are not well suited to lead at GE, especially when they are unable or unwilling to act in concert with GE's (equally explicit and simple) values and principles. The personal honesty about oneself and others, which is a hallmark of individual GE leaders, reflects and spreads candour throughout this large multinational corporation.

Simplicity and clarity are also evident in Professor Debashis Chatterjee's essay on collective meaning in Chapter 18. He describes the guiding principle espoused and applied by Kumar Mangalam Birla, founder and chairman of India's huge and extremely successful multinational conglomerate, the Aditya Birla Group:

> "Our philosophy is that we want to be the last man standing. That is, we want to be among the lowest-cost producers in the world so that when the product cycle is down, we are still competitive."

Again, you can imagine that Birla's personal drive for success has shown up in his company's competitiveness.

These simple ideas focus on varied themes, but each is consistent with former P&G CEO A.G. Lafley's advice to keep things personal and "Sesame Street simple". These ideas guide thousands of decisions and actions in these diverse companies. And each would be simplistic and hollow rhetoric if uttered by leaders who did not personally live the story they were creating and who lacked deep understanding of the business and people they led. The lesson for leaders is that your leadership agenda will create your company's story if it is based on your deep experience, including instructive mistakes and failures, that you have earned the hard way and then work to explain and show what you learned to other leaders in simple, authentic and emotionally compelling ways.

So, for aspiring leaders, our advice is to create a personal leadership agenda that comes from the core of your identity. This personal agenda can lead to profoundly simple ideas that will shape your organisation's vision and purpose with deep and broad effects.

2. HR Issues are Essential to Your Effectiveness, Regardless of the Influence of the HR Function in Your Company

There is considerable variance in the amount of influence that the HR function wields in Asian companies, as in the rest of the world. In some places, senior HR executives have great influence over everything: from the company's overall strategy to promotion decisions involving the most senior executives. At the other end of the spectrum, HR is viewed as a largely transactional and compliance function, even a necessary evil. This unfortunate attitude is usually conveyed in a subtle fashion, such as through failure to consult HR executives during major decisions, infrequent contact with the CEO, or not investing in innovative HR practices. There are times, however, when such disrespect can be quite explicit. One HR manager in a very successful US company (with a large and growing presence in Asia) decided to leave her company when the CEO told a gathering of HR managers and executives: "You are just like barnacles on a ship; all you do is slow us down." Or as Michael Jenkins reported in Chapter 29 on leadership transition:

> "One Chinese CEO, an entrepreneur running an 80-strong organisation in Beijing, once shared the following philosophy: 'I don't see what is so difficult about managing the leadership transition. All you have to do is identify the top performers, tell them what you want from them and manage them closely. If they hit their targets, they get to stay. If they don't, they get shown the door. And you just hire in other people who *can* do the job.' "

This CEO's statement, of course, is a dangerous over-simplification. It assumes that human abilities are fixed and developing leaders is a waste of time, and it masks the

299

complexity and skill required to differentiate the best from the worst performers. It also implies an unlimited supply of top talent, even though every participant in our Roundtable lamented how increasingly difficult it was to find people with top skills and potential in Asia. In contrast, enlightened Asian companies, which are likely to trump competitors in the long run, take an opposite approach. Again, Jenkins provides an instructive example:

> "Forward-looking companies, such as Samsung in Korea, have created fantastic systems for online learning, self-assessment and ongoing leadership development support that meet organisational requirements while simultaneously meeting the development needs of the individual."

Similarly, the role of HR takes centrestage in Cordelia Chung's description of IBM's Expertise Taxonomy System:

> "a company-wide database available on a website. It establishes a common language for all the different job roles, associated skills and competencies used across all business units in the company."

Yet, regardless of whether HR is viewed as a powerful and respected function, or a powerless if necessary nuisance, the domain of skills and knowledge embraced by HR are among the most crucial elements for building and sustaining a successful business. Again, take a look at the list of eight institutional success factors that this book is organised around. HR practices are key to both leadership and organisation success. As the unfortunate quote from the Chinese CEO suggests, an executive may know an individual who is talented and can be moved into a key job. However, without embedded HR practices, each decision is an isolated event, not a sustained pattern. Embedded HR practices enable knowledge to spread throughout a company about the hallmarks of effective leaders and to be remembered and applied systematically. Moreover, by focusing on patterns rather than treating each hiring, evaluation, promotion decision as a unique and isolated event, it is far easier to learn from past failures and successes, thus avoiding the all too common tendency for companies to repeat the same mistakes again and again.

HR's expertise is equally important to other success factors, such as creating customer-centred actions. For example, at the Far East Organization, customer service training, subsidised trips for employees throughout Asia to learn about the nuances of different cities and national cultures, and instruction in foreign languages all reflect HR skills and contribution. Finally, most of the successful strategies implemented by Asian companies described here could not be implemented without aligning, integrating and innovating HR practices. Singapore Airlines's impressive track record of being both a service and a cost leader (which depends heavily on intensive training and coaching), and GE's "competencies in technology and innovation" that enabled the company to rapidly develop and sell medical scanners in lower income markets in Asia, both come from persistent and wise investments in HR practices.

The upshot is that, regardless of whether your company's HR function is powerful or powerless, if you want to be an effective leader, you need to spend a great deal of your time and emotional energy on "people" issues. We learned this lesson after decades of teaching, consulting and studying successful managers. In particular, we see one recurring pattern: aspiring and new managers often have little interest or patience with such issues; they routinely trivialise "people problems" as mushy and distracting issues that distract from "real" business challenges in areas such as finance and strategy. But the more senior the management audience or individual leader, the more interest they have in such "human" issues and the more crucial they believe such issues are to their organisation's performance. One of the most frequent comments that we hear from CEOs and Executive Vice-Presidents is that they wish they had understood how important such issues were earlier in their careers. Indeed, even Apple's Steve Jobs, who has historically shown little interest in leadership development, personally enticed Yale School of Management Dean Joel Podolny to leave his post and to run "Apple University", which is focused on training, mentoring and coaching Apple's future leaders. And to convey the message that Apple University is a top priority, Jobs located Podolny's office on executive row, right between his own office and Chief Operating Officer Tim Cook's office.

So, aspiring leaders need to attend to aligned and innovative HR practices that reflect customers' expectations. You may want to upgrade the quality of your HR organisation and expect your HR professionals to contribute to business opportunities and challenges.

3. Persistence and a Touch of Impatience are a Potent Combination

These two intertwined (and nearly contradictory) themes were usually left unsaid, but in hearing the CEOs' and CHROs' talk, and in reading their essays, this blend was always palpable to us. Consider, for example, the "can-do" spirit that is a hallmark of the DBS culture and that pervades the two essays about this bank. The story about Subir Chakraborty, Puneet Punj and Sandeep Kumar (see Chapter 2), part of the DBS India team, demonstrated persistence — and more than a bit of impatience — as they travelled through floods, downed trees and traffic jams to meet with an important new client. The customer was most impressed and relationship flourished, after "our customer saw his bankers dripping wet, with shoes in one hand and documents in another!" The "can-do" spirit of DBS is also evident in the late nights and weekends that DBS employees devoted to the 40/40 project in 2008 (see Chapter 16). As their essay reports:

> "as DBS celebrated our 40th anniversary, we challenged our people to develop 40 community initiatives, to be completed in 40 days, which would impact underprivileged children in the area of learning."

This programme was so successful, and the can-do spirit was so strong, that it had to be renamed the 80/40 project as DBS employees ended up completing twice as many projects in the 40 days then first planned. Ultimately, 1,300 DBS employees pitched in and completed projects in 11 countries, such as raising funds for a new learning centre for children in Vietnam.

Of course, most examples of persistence with a bit of impatience were less dramatic than these DBS stories. But we saw evidence of this blend in Richard Kelly's talk at the Roundtable about his mission to bring creativity techniques, along with creative confidence, to the leaders, companies and government agencies that his people worked with throughout Asia. This combination is similarly evident in GE's "In China, For China" initiative, which has been part of a long-term effort to understand and operate in effective and respectful ways in that Asian country. This initiative has included hiring over 12,000 Chinese employees in recent years, establishing the Global Research Center in Shanghai (to develop environmentally friendly technologies), and signing an agreement with Tsinghua University to produce research for GE's ecomagination initiative.

The commitment to a long-term time perspective is evident in these and so many other examples of effective leadership in Asia presented in this book and discussed in the Roundtable. These leaders are successful, in part, because they see themselves as running a marathon rather than a sprint. But this ability to take the long-term view is coupled with palpable impatience, a kind of relentless restlessness, that drives people to keep doing things just a little faster, work just a little harder, be just a little smarter, and do things just a little bit better than in the past — and a little better than competing firms. Such persistence and impatience, which has been especially evident during the impressive rise of local and multinational firms throughout Asia during the past 20 years, is a hallmark of the leaders discussed in this book and of the mindset that experienced and successful leaders throughout the world pass on to newcomers to the craft. As one senior executive once put it to us, "I try to teach my managers the art of creating urgency without acting like life is one long emergency."

So, aspiring leaders need to find the right mix of patience and persistence, short- and long-term thinking. To manage this paradox, you need to recognise your predisposition (to either patience or persistence) and then force yourself to recognise the other side. Or, you might encourage the short- versus long-term debate among your team members so that trade-offs are public. Or, you might work to more fully connect your short-term actions to long-term aspirations.

4. Learning to "Read" Situations and Adjust Your Leadership Style is One of the Most Crucial and Difficult Skills to Develop

The notion that there is one best leadership style for every situation has been rejected by both researchers and practitioners for many years (Bass, 1990). Indeed, recent writings and research emphasise that a hallmark of the best leaders is their ability to adjust their style in response to different situations, and to make adjustments on the fly in response to the reactions of followers, peers and superiors (Sutton, 2010). In particular, recent research by Ames and Flynn (2007) shows that the best leaders are rated by followers as moderately assertive — as neither too overbearing nor too soft. These researchers go on to emphasise that their research does not just mean that the best bosses always convey the same level of assertiveness; rather, it means they have the sensitivity to understand situational differences (and signs that they are being either too assertive or not assertive enough). And this is coupled with the skill and flexibility they need to increase or decrease their level of assertiveness as required.

This research dovetails well with the themes that emerged during the Roundtable and that are emphasised in several essays in this book. Deb Henretta's piece in Chapter 28 emphasises that there is no "one-size-fits-all" leadership style for Asian leaders. She explains that P&G works to provide its leaders with a deep understanding of differences between Asian and non-Asian cultures (as well as local differences among Asian cultures and countries) to help them be knowledgeable, flexible and skilled enough to engage in appropriate "style switching". Following Ames and Flynn's research, many of the examples offered by leaders who attended the Roundtable focused on understanding when it is wise to become more versus less assertive. Henretta provides a vivid example in Chapter 28:

> "a Japanese leader will need to adapt to a more direct style as he/she interacts with an Australian manager and then return to a more indirect style when interacting with a Thai peer."

Along similar lines, another recent study suggests that expressing anger is likely to be an effective strategy when negotiating with people from Western countries, but typically backfires when negotiating with people from East Asian countries. The researchers suggest that anger is seen as a sign of seriousness and toughness by most Westerners, but East Asians see anger as a sign that a person cannot control their emotions (Shirako and Maddux, 2010).

This research suggests that as leaders mature, they keep building and becoming more adept at using a repertoire of skills that can be adapted to fit diverse situations. Early entrants in almost any profession have a narrow range of abilities and their success is determined by how quickly they can gain breadth. Actors, architects, lawyers, psychologists and teachers all need to expand the ways they work with clients. The broader their skills, the more clients they will have — and the better they will serve each client. Leadership is no different. New leaders usually begin their jobs with narrow skill sets; but the best quickly realise they need to build a far broader range of skills, which drives them to learn to lead different people, settings and contexts, and to develop the flexibility and observational skills that enable them to "turn on" and "turn off" the right approaches at the right time.

If you combine the experience of companies, such as P&G, with recent research on the most effective bosses, it is clear that the ability to do "style switching" is crucial in Asia. As Asian organisations expand into the global environment, Asian leaders will need to broaden their leadership skills. This breadth becomes visible as Asian leaders need the ability to understand when (and how) to be direct, assertive and even show a flash of anger versus when it is best to be indirect and subtle, press your point gently (or say nothing at all) and keep your temper in check. The findings by Ames and Flynn suggest that learning to be "perfectly assertive" is among the most important hallmarks of a great leader, for example, more important than charisma. As Asian leaders begin to play in more diverse, complex and global organisations, their repertoire of skills must also expand.

Having a broad leadership range does not mean the leader cannot be authentic and true to himself or herself. While there are some common elements all competent leaders must demonstrate (Ulrich et al, 2008), Asian leaders may lead from very different styles. For example, if your unchecked "authentic self" consistently offends others and makes it difficult to work well with others, you might be wise (for your own good and the good of your organisation) to develop the interpersonal sensitivity and emotional control that is necessary for becoming an effective leader.

In short, aspiring leaders need to realise that their entry level leadership skills will have to expand for them to continue to lead effectively. You cannot rely on the skills you had when you were selected as a leader to stay an effective leader. As Marshall Goldsmith (2007) puts it: "What got you here, won't get you there." You need to learn to lead different people, projects, situations and outcomes. As you assume demanding and new tasks, your leadership breadth will increase and you will become more effective at this challenging and crucial craft.

5. Creating Unity of Purpose and Collective Understanding is a Job that Never Ends

This was one of the most frequent and persistent themes in our Roundtable discussions. It is also raised explicitly in several pieces in this volume and is an implicit theme in most others. Most of the leaders we heard from and about devote enormous time and energy to explaining *what* goals, values and strategies are and ought to be shared by the people they lead, *why* such collective understandings are so crucial to everyone's success and happiness, and *how* to achieve and sustain such shared understandings and focused efforts. In this regard, leaders become meaning makers who not only master the motions of leadership, but inspire emotional attachment and personal contributions among those they lead (Ulrich and Ulrich, 2010).

This theme is evident in the HR practices used by companies, including the Far East Organization, IBM, GE, P&G and MediaCorp, to select, train, reward and promote — and, in some cases, remove — employees. In all these companies, such practices are explicitly used to instill understanding and guide actions that bolster unity of purpose and create meaning for employees. GE is especially interesting in this regard. The company has operated in Asia for a long time and has customised products, management practices, pricing policies and other attributes to fit local cultures and conditions. Yet, the company has such clear values and powerful supporting practices that leaders involved in the Roundtable emphasised that the GE culture is so strong that it trumps country or regional culture by a large margin in shaping how GE employees in Asia (and the rest of the world) think and act on the job.

The essays by DBS leaders on customers and on inspiring collective meaning demonstrate a commitment to espousing and explaining collective understanding and goals, and then creating paths so that people can band together to achieve a unity of purpose. The commitment of the senior management to improve customer experience, for example, animated a host of initiatives reflecting the desire to put DBS employees in "our customer's shoes". These include a determined effort to simplify the language used in communication with clients. The aim is to avoid banking and legal jargon and to get rid of the "fine print", whenever possible. This collective purpose is also seen in their programme to help older customers who prefer to walk to branches rather than do their banking via the Internet. They hired 120 DBS retirees to help older customers with their banking transactions. This focus on customer experience also helped to inspire a programme that provoked over 600 suggestions on ways that DBS could work more effectively. The point, as the DBS case shows, is that when leaders express clear goals and values, they also need to provide avenues — programmes, resources, expertise and procedures — that enable people to turn their leader's words and their collective aspirations into action.

Actions by senior leaders can be especially important for reinforcing unity of purpose, shaping a shared identity and injecting collective beliefs into values, strategies and routines. To return to DBS, senior leaders are not just talking about the importance of customer service; they now spend chunks of time interacting directly with customers at call centres and branches. Similarly, senior executives in P&G Asia do not just talk about learning how to lead in culturally sensitive ways through "style switching". The two P&G leaders (one from a Western background, the other from an East Asian background) who attended the Roundtable explained how they modelled such "switching" during meetings, which showed their colleagues how it was done and encouraged them to follow suit. Finally, it was pretty easy for MediaCorp CEO, Lucas Chow, to talk about the importance of putting people first. But when financial pressures hit MediaCorp during the worldwide financial crisis in 2008, this espoused value was really put to the test. Mr Chow and his senior team responded by implementing unpaid "MediaCorp Day Offs" throughout the company, which saved many jobs. This was a crucial turning point because, as Mr Chow explained:

> "My senior management team and I were given the opportunity to turn a difficult business decision to one that increased the level of trust by a quantum leap across the organisation."

The upshot is that creating unity of purpose and collective understanding often starts with inspiring and comforting words that are uttered by senior leaders or produced by staffers in human resources, corporate communications or elsewhere. Yet, such words are dangerous when they are hollow — when not backed by systems, expertise, resources and leader's decisions and actions. They are dangerous because they breed cynicism and lack of faith in leaders and organisations. Wise leaders learn to walk a fine line between promising more than they or the company, as a whole, can deliver versus setting inspirational stretch goals that will inspire collective action. Wise leaders also know that unity of purpose is not something they can create once or can sustain through an occasional speech, a programme that lasts a couple of months and is then forgotten, by throwing a party for employees every now and then, or assigning a powerless senior executive to the role. The collective trust and effort that are hallmarks of true unity of purpose can only be maintained through persistent and visible action by senior leaders. To paraphrase one senior executive we work with:

> "You've got to realise that they are watching you very closely. They can smell your hypocrisy from a mile away, and once they do, they won't do much for you or the company."

Aspiring leaders who strive to create unity of purpose and collective understanding can start the journey by answering a series of personal and organisational questions: who am I? What are my strengths and how can I use them to serve others? What is my purpose and what is the collective purpose of my organisation? How can I articulate and communicate this purpose to those inside and outside my organisation? How do I create a sense of meaning and purpose for my employees that will impact customers, investors and communities where we work? As leaders honestly address with these more affective and personal questions, they go beyond behavioural commitment to an emotional commitment that bonds employees (and themselves) to their organisations.

Conclusion

This book has focused on the four questions and eight success factors for leaders. This framework captures the institutionalisation of leadership and offers leaders a chance to build leadership within their companies. Yet, we do not want to ignore the personal elements of leadership. The five points we make in ending this book are essential elements that aspiring leaders should know and do to earn the right to be called — and see themselves — as successful. By attending to both institutional and individual leadership challenges, Asian leaders need no longer be in place by accident, but by intent. When leadership investments are targeted on these eight success factors, we believe that not only will leaders be more effective, but also their organisations.

In the next decade, we envision leadership insights from Asian settings having a broader impact in leadership as it is practised, conceptualised and studied. The growth of Asia is so rapid and the demands so great that Asian leaders will invent new approaches to tackle the questions we raise. Their actions and insights will likely set the tone for how effective leaders throughout the world think and act. If Asia can be the leadership sandbox for the next decade, the ideas in this book may become the prologue for leadership in the future that will benefit business, non-profit and government leaders and organisations around the globe.

References

Ames, D.R. and F.J. Flynn. (2007). What breaks a leader: the curvilinear relation between assertiveness and leadership. *Journal of Personality and Social Psychology*, 92:307–24.

Bass, B.M. (1990). *Bass and Stogdill's Handbook of Leadership* (3rd edition). New York: Free Press.

Goldsmith, M. (2007). *What Got You Here Won't Get You There*. New York: Hyperion.

Schutz, W. (1979). *Profound Simplicity: Foundations for a Social Philosophy*. New York: Pfeiffer & Co.

Shirako, A. and W.W. Maddux. (2010). Cultural variance in the interpersonal effects of anger in negotiations. *Psychological Science*, 21:882–9.

Sutton, R.I. (2010). *Good Boss, Bad Boss*. New York: Business Plus.

Ulrich, D., N. Smallwood and K. Sweetman. (2008). *Leadership Code: Five Rules to Lead By*. Boston: Harvard Business School Press.

Ulrich, D. and W.L. Ulrich. (2010). *The Why of Work*. New York: McGraw-Hill.

Index